GIS *for* Health Organizations

Laura Lang

ESRI Press

Published by
Environmental Systems Research Institute, Inc.
380 New York Street
Redlands, California 92373-8100

Environmental Systems Research Institute, Inc.

GIS for Health Organizations
ISBN 1-879102-65-X

Contents

Preface

Since the 1997 appearance of Andy Mitchell's *Zeroing In,* ESRI Press has published several books about how real people in a variety of specific industries use geographic information system (GIS) technology to manage their increasingly complex and diverse activities. For the most part, all of these case-study books have covered activities one would naturally associate with GIS: routing emergency vehicles, siting new businesses, managing networks (whether pipelines or phone lines or freeway systems), and preserving natural resources, to name only a few. All of these activities have an obvious connection to geography: they all have to do with place and with the objects that move (or don't move) within that place.

With *GIS for Health Organizations,* we begin to traverse some less-obvious uses for GIS. Sure, health planners use GIS for tasks similar to those already detailed: siting new hospitals or clinics, determining market areas, keeping track of room assignments in a large hospital. But these uses, surprisingly enough, are not the earliest uses of GIS in health care, nor are they, at the time of this publication, the most common uses.

For that, we have to go all the way back to 1849 and Dr. John Snow's research into the causes of the cholera epidemic in London. The maps he made showing the pattern of cholera victims in the neighborhood of one well constitute a classic use of geographic information to draw epidemiological conclusions. And GIS, in the strictly formal sense of computer software programs, continues to help medical science understand the causes of disease and how it spreads. It is even used, as you will soon read, to predict the spread of a toxic chemical released by an early-morning train wreck, and to identify the people who rate being evacuated first because of their sensitivity to this chemical.

It is my hope that GIS will soon be as integral to the effective management of health care resources as it already is to natural resource management, transportation, utilities, and so many other important fields of human endeavor.

Will GIS software help people live healthier, happier lives? Read on, and judge for yourself. Whatever you decide, this book is dedicated to your very good health.

Jack Dangermond
President, ESRI

Acknowledgments

Health care is one of the fastest-growing customer segments at ESRI. The excitement among our health experts, and their users, is contagious.

The idea to write this book came from Bill Miller, former director of ESRI® Educational Services. Soon after the arrival of Bill Davenhall, ESRI's Health Solutions Group manager, user sites were selected that would illustrate the broad range of scientific, business, and patient care applications across a wide variety of health organizations.

Bill Davenhall was very patient in guiding the development of each chapter and keeping the book on track. He was aided by a very devoted Health Solutions team including Ann Bossard, Laura Feaster, Jennifer Harar, Peggy Harper, and Bill Hoffman. These professionals work on the "front lines," meeting with prospective customers, designing and implementing systems, and maintaining great customer relations, and immediately recognized this book's potential in helping to spread the word about GIS to more organizations.

There would be no book without the many fantastic people, pioneers in this growing field, who generously shared their knowledge about the projects described in these pages. While they are acknowledged individually at the end of each chapter, I would like to take this opportunity to again tell them how grateful I am for their help and encouragement throughout this project. They made this project a wonderful career experience for me, and I am very lucky to have worked with each and every one of them.

Finally, thanks to the great team at ESRI Press. Contributing to the smooth sailing of this text were Lisa Godin, project editor; Michael Karman, editor; Michael Hyatt, book designer, production artist, and copy editor; and Gina Davidson, cover designer. Barbara Shaeffer reviewed the text from a legal perspective, and Cliff Crabbe oversaw print production.

The management team at ESRI Press, including Christian Harder, Judy Boyd, and, of course, Bill Miller, were important backers of this project. Special thanks also needs to be extended to Jack Dangermond, who always listens to new ideas—and usually says yes—and his wife and ESRI vice president, Laura Dangermond. Without you two, and your wonderful company, books like this would not be written.

In keeping with Jack's vision and drive, we hope this book, like its predecessors in the growing ESRI Press Case Studies Series, helps more organizations open their doors to the promise of GIS.

Chapter 1

•••••• Beyond epidemiology

MEDICAL GEOGRAPHY, the study of how disease and health care are distributed across the face of the earth, is nothing new. For hundreds of years, scientists have researched the connections between health and the environment. Now they have a new tool—GIS.

Epidemiology, the most familiar type of geographic study in medicine, maps the progress of diseases, famines, toxic spills, and other health disasters. But another type of study, health care facilities surveys, is becoming increasingly important as competition for business increases. These surveys determine how many of a specific type of facility currently exist in an area, find the best locations for new ones, and determine how many to open.

In the larger medical community, hospital administrators, pharmaceutical companies, managed care providers, and long-term care providers are just starting to use GIS. For these people, GIS offers enormous potential for improving their services by organizing, using, and distributing spatial information.

A geographic information system (GIS) is a computer system for analyzing and mapping just about anything, moving or stationary. A GIS integrates common database operations, such as query and statistical analysis, with the ability to see how data relates in space and time. The maps produced with a GIS are useful for showing places and the events that occur there, like outbreaks of disease. They are useful for analyzing and visualizing any system that's spatial, for mapping a patient's heart or brain, for instance, or showing a breakdown of diagnoses on a map of the body, or even indicating which beds on a hospital floor are occupied, for how long, and by whom.

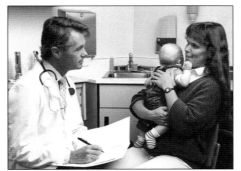

Today's technology has not only given health care professionals more effective medicines and better equipment, it has also given them GIS, a tool that helps them manage information.

What GIS does

A GIS manages spatial information—
information about locations and their
physical relations to each other, information about things that move through
space, whether animals, humans, or
clouds of poisonous gas. Because it
combines information about where
things are with information about what
those things are, a GIS can even be said
to produce knowledge.

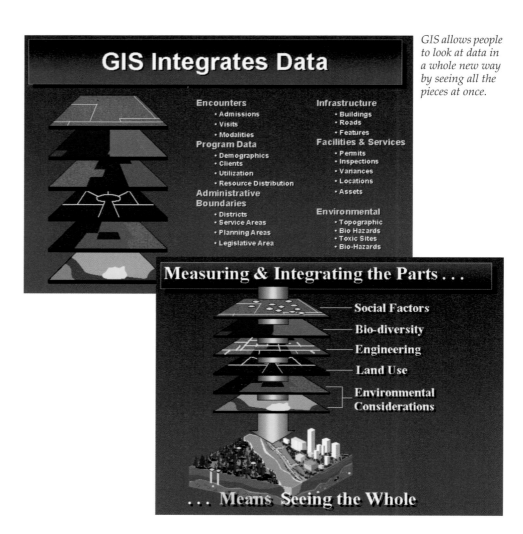

*GIS allows people
to look at data in
a whole new way
by seeing all the
pieces at once.*

Who uses it: public health organizations

The Centers for Disease Control (CDC), the world's premier disease-tracking organization, has used GIS for at least a decade to study how disease spreads from place to place and to study how toxic substances affect people's health.

The Dartmouth Medical School's CD–ROM uses GIS technology to show how the amount and type of health care services Americans receive depend greatly on where they live—on both the capacity of the health care system in their area and on the methods practiced by local doctors. Differences in how often hospitals are used, variations in how care of the terminally ill is delivered, and patterns of elective surgery raise important questions about the consequences and value of health care.

The work of these health GIS pioneers has encouraged a growing number of state and local agencies to publish their health statistics, using GIS to provide access to that data on the Internet or on intranets.

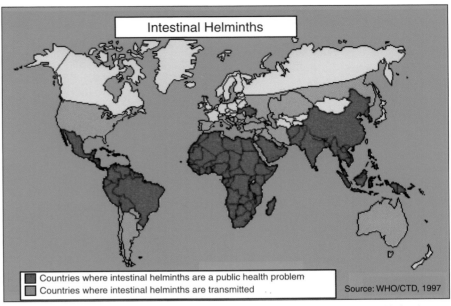

The World Health Organization's Division of the Control of Tropical Diseases publishes its statistics on the World Wide Web. Visitors can view these statistics on a map, like this one showing the geographical distribution of intestinal parasites worldwide.

Who uses it: health planners

Health planners use GIS to assess how well patients are served by doctors and staff at any individual site, and whether they had to drive too far to get there. Knowing which services different populations typically need, and how far away the services are, health planners can use GIS to anticipate demand for any particular service.

Recently, health planners have used GIS to evaluate marketing programs, make siting decisions, and figure out how best to allocate health services. The maps they create may help them see, for example, where there is room for a new facility.

More and more consumers are turning to the Internet to find a hospital, a specialist, a nursing home, a 24-hour pharmacy, a mental health therapist, a chiropractor, or any other provider or service, but the same maps available on the Web can help prospective patients find the closest center. More and more Internet sites are being engineered with GIS to provide accurate and timely information that can be found by just pointing and clicking on locations on a map.

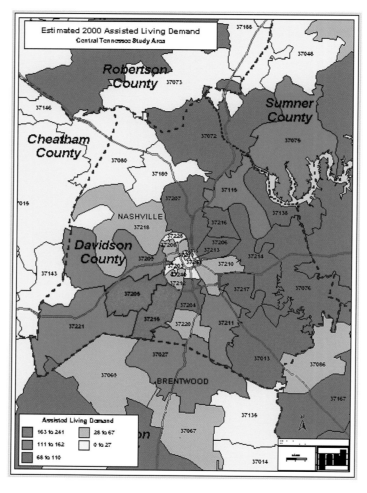

With geographic information systems, health planners can more effectively demonstrate their market by mapping their patients or the population in general.

Who uses it: business managers

Health managers use GIS to evaluate prospective sites for hospital or outpatient clinics. They use it to tell sales teams which physicians are most likely to try a new drug or service (and provide a driving map to their offices), or send health services to people's homes by the most efficient routes.

Armed with a client's data and some data of their own, the marketing and planning consultants can determine the exact mix of products and services that best meet that client's needs. They can also determine whether their client is spending too much or too little for their health care, and whether they are focusing their preventive efforts in the right areas.

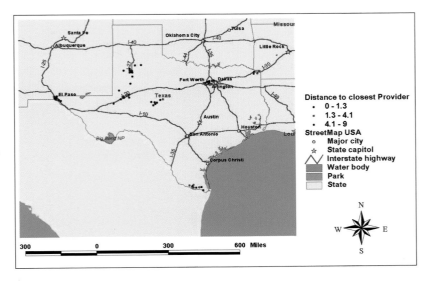

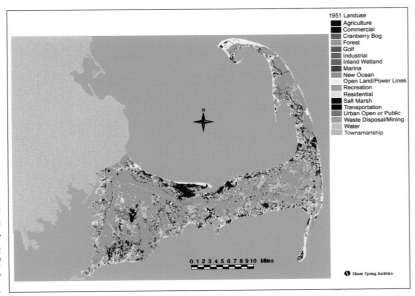

Once information about land use or where patients live is imported into the GIS, it can be used to gain insight into both clinical and business issues facing health organizations.

Who uses it: large health organizations

Even in a relatively small community hospital, there may be upward of 40 separate applications that make up the organization's information system. Most hospitals and managed care organizations recognize the value of GIS with their planning and marketing operations, and practically every health organization has applications such as patient registration.

The newest trend is hospitals working to integrate all their various systems. It's not uncommon to have many different brands of software running the various departments' systems and more than one hardware platform. Integrating all these systems means easier access to the data, making it easier for different departments to cooperate. Programs like ArcView® GIS make it easy to integrate data from a variety of sources and work with the data geographically, which allows hospitals to get more from their data by using it in new ways.

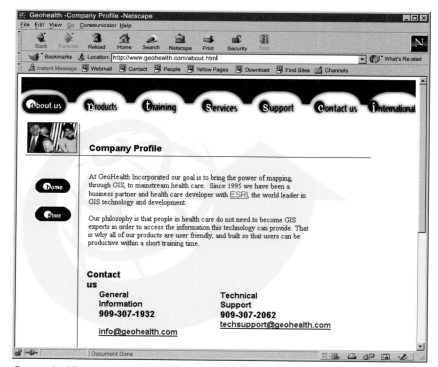

Companies like GeoHealth specialize in integrating geographic information systems, offering hospitals and health care administrators a custom mapping application for their company's internal use or one that they can market under their organization's name.

Who uses it: insurance companies

Insurance companies' involvement in the medical world goes much farther than just paying the bills. They use GIS to make sure their members are within reasonable distances of the services they need.

Many large health insurance companies have developed enormous data warehouses containing demographic data, as well as geographic attributes of specific diseases, interventions, and treatments. Knowing the demographics of an area, which health problems are prevalent there, and how they can be treated successfully, may help managed care organizations like Kaiser Permanente decide how much money they'll need to spend to run a center successfully and where to build new facilities.

Primary Care Travel Time Areas and Members

150,000 Members

340,000 Members

A

B

C

165,000 Members

Kaiser Permanente, Southern California, uses GIS to evaluate member distribution when deciding how much money to allocate to each hospital and where to open new facilities.

Who uses it: practically everyone else

Pharmaceutical companies are finding that GIS helps them target the physicians most likely to use their product. And they can make more balanced sales territories and more efficient routes as well with the use of GIS.

Building contractors use GIS to help health care companies decide where to locate new clinics and decide how big those facilities need to be to serve everyone well.

Manufacturers of medical equipment use GIS to find out which diseases and conditions are most common in an area so they know which of their products to market there.

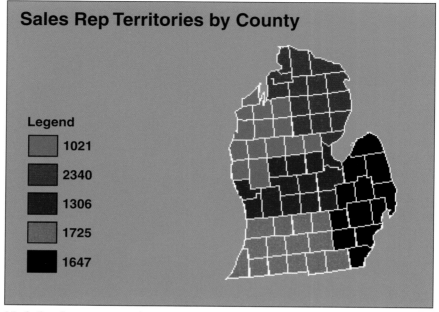

Marketing departments can increase productivity by using GIS to balance sales territories among their representatives.

The future of GIS in health

Hospitals may soon be able to use GIS to create real-time maps that track the movement of their personnel and patients. By being able to accurately monitor the movements of employees and those that are registered as patients, hospitals can better guarantee safety and security, especially in sensitive departments, like the maternity ward.

With more than 230 infectious diseases distributed throughout 200 countries, it's becoming increasingly difficult for researchers to accurately monitor their spread. The patterns of these diseases, some of them new, some reemerging, some ongoing, and others disappearing, change from area to area and season to season. By the time accurate research can be completed, the results are often outdated. With GIS, researchers will be able to publish this data immediately.

The continual advance of Internet technology makes it the chosen medium for publishing and distributing GIS data. A large part of the power of GIS is the ability to share results in an easy-to-understand, visual medium. The outlook for GIS in the health disciplines appears unlimited.

Tomorrow's applications of GIS in the health care industry go beyond managing patient data or analyzing market information. Increasing security, finding ways to release up-to-the-minute information, and providing access to a wider variety of information on the Internet are just a few of the ways GIS will change health care.

The case studies

The 11 chapters that follow feature a variety of health care organizations. Each demonstrates a specific application of GIS in the health care industry.

Through these examples, you'll see how the common thread of geography has enabled these organizations to use their data in new ways. By integrating spatial data from various departments, they've been able to increase efficiency, improve service, and sometimes even save lives.

Chapter 2

Starting with the classics

IN THE MID-19TH CENTURY, death and despair engulfed London. In the Soho district, when nearly six hundred people died from cholera in just 10 days, death tolls rang around the clock from the church bell tower. With no known cure, panic spread throughout the city. Dr. John Snow, a London physician, knew that to contain the disease, they would have to find the source. Using maps showing the locations of water pumps and the homes of people who died of cholera, Snow was able to show that one pump was causing most of the disease.

To find the geographical sources of disease, public health officials still use maps, just as Snow did. With GIS, however, today's researchers have a significant advantage. This chapter shows how the Centers for Disease Control and Prevention (CDC) provides researchers with software so they can use GIS spatial analysis and modeling functions to support epidemiology, using data from Dr. John Snow's classic medical mapping study.

The CDC's Epidemiology Program Office in Atlanta, Georgia, coordinates public health surveillance in the United States and throughout the rest of the world. As part of this effort, the office trains public health experts in the use of Epi Info 2000 and Epi Map 2000, GIS software developed by the CDC and distributed at its Web site (www.cdc.gov).

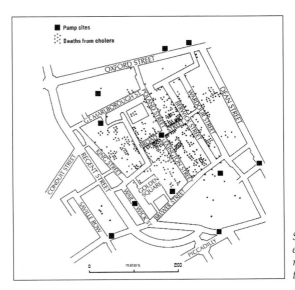

Snow's cholera maps, famous in epidemiological circles, are familiar to researchers and help them understand the power of mapping their study data.

145,000 copies

Epi Info 2000 provides tools for creating charts and graphs and conducting statistical analyses with field data. Epi Map 2000, developed with MapObjects® software from ESRI, displays data from Epi Info (or from dBASE® files) as maps.

Previous releases of both Epi Map and Epi Info for DOS have been distributed in 15 languages and are already used by more than 145,000 public health professionals in 117 countries around the world. To introduce this audience to the Microsoft® Windows® version of these programs, the CDC has developed new course materials using Dr. Snow's cholera maps. Sample data from Snow's classic medical mapping study is included in the tutorial exercise.

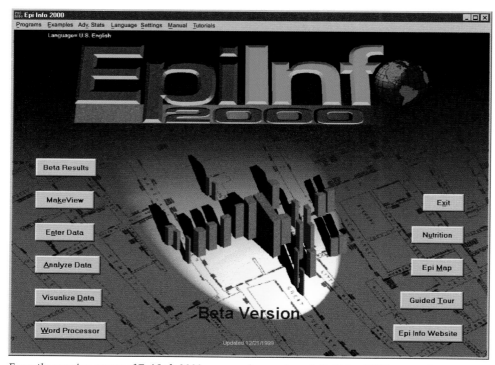

From the opening screen of Epi Info 2000, a researcher can launch Epi Map 2000, a mapping application built with MapObjects software.

Proving his theory

In 1849, Dr. Snow published a pamphlet, *On the Mode of Communication of Cholera,* which stated that cholera was a contagious disease transmitted mainly through contaminated drinking water.

When an outbreak occurred in the Soho district in 1854, Snow found further evidence to support his theory. He began by showing that cholera occurred mostly in customers of the Southwark and Vauxhall water company, which drew its water from the lower Thames River, polluted with London sewage. Just before the outbreak, the Lambeth Water Company had relocated its water source to the upper Thames, above the contamination.

Snow's theory that cholera came from contaminated water differed from a commonly held theory that diseases were transmitted by inhaling vapors.

Calming fears

At the peak of the epidemic, more than five hundred people in one neighborhood died from cholera in just 10 days. Residents there began to panic, thinking that they were somehow being infected by the buried corpses of plague victims who died during the European pandemic a century before. Housing had been built on the cemetery where those plague victims were buried. As cholera deaths occurred in these homes, and in homes surrounding the area, the residents feared that they were being infected by vapors coming from the ground. To reassure these people, Snow created a map of the neighborhood, showing that no more people got cholera near the cemetery than anywhere else.

They could see on this map that cholera deaths were not confined to the area around the cemetery.

The 1854 Soho outbreak allowed Snow to test his theory by mapping the two components for comparison. Students use historical data from an Epi Info 2000 database file to re-create Snow's maps as they work through the CDC software tutorial. This data contains the locations of deaths and pumps and has been especially formatted for this exercise.

As shown here, the resulting map visually displays the 1854 cholera deaths as small black circles. The former burial plot is an underlying green polygon.

The Broad Street pump

Dr. Snow created other maps to show why so many deaths had happened in that particular neighborhood. He was able to see that most cases centered around Broad Street, specifically the Broad Street pump.

On the map they have already created, the students overlay the positions of the area's water pumps, the only source of drinking water at that time. With Epi Info's Analysis program, they calculate the mean distance between each of the pumps and the cholera victims. The measurements confirm that most of the 578 cholera victims are clustered around a single well.

Snow used his water pump map to advise a skeptical but desperate assembly of officials to have the pump handle at Cambridge and Broad streets removed. This way they could test whether or not cholera was spread by that pump's water. After the handle was removed, the number of cholera cases dropped dramatically.

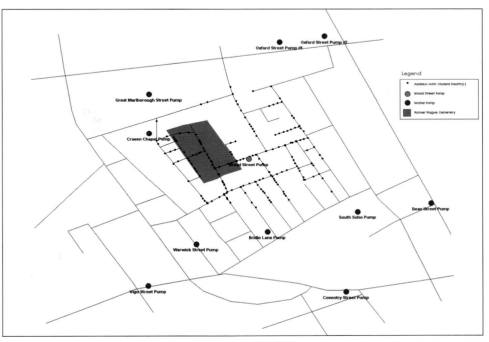

The Broad Street pump (red) proved to be the source of contaminated water, just as Snow had thought.

Working in today's world

Once they become familiar with how to analyze and display study results from Snow's historical cholera study, students can start substituting their own project data, using Epi Info to enter counts, rates, or other numeric values and Epi Map to display and analyze the data. Whether a disease is infectious or chronic, maps are valuable tools for their investigations.

Using GIS, they can search for spatial relationships—homing in on the source of salmonella poisoning, Legionnaire's disease, or toxic exposures. By mapping demographic factors like housing type or age in relation to disease conditions, they can predict target populations for a disease and fund programs to prevent its spread.

As researchers worldwide download Epi Info 2000 and Epi Map 2000, they will be able to apply the power of spatial analysis to their projects and visualize their data in new ways.

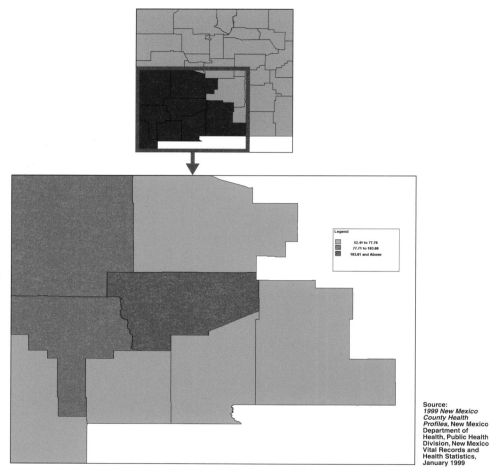

Source:
1999 New Mexico County Health Profiles, New Mexico Department of Health, Public Health Division, New Mexico Vital Records and Health Statistics, January 1999

This map displays YPLL data from the Border Epidemiology and Environmental Health Center of the Border Health Office, which focuses its work on New Mexico "District 3" counties. YPLL is the measure of the number of years of potential life lost by each death occurring before reaching average life expectancy. Choropleth maps like this can guide and focus public health program attention.

The system

Hardware: PCs running Microsoft Windows 95®, Windows 98®, and Windows NT®

Software: Epi Map 2000 and Epi Info 2000 (to be released in early 2000)

The data

Epi Map was developed with MapObjects software and includes MapObjects data (streets, highways, census boundaries, ZIP Codes, counties, states, and countries). Plague data and streets of old London were re-created by the development team using Dr. Snow's maps and historical writings.

The people

Special thanks to Dr. Andrew G. Dean, Thomas G. Arner, and Catherine Schenck–Yglesias of the CDC's Epidemiology Program Office, and to Andrew Dent of EDS.

Chapter 3

•••••• Finding the link

BREAST CANCER—we don't know what causes it, or how to prevent it. But recently, some scientists have speculated that estrogen-like chemicals in the environment, called endocrine disrupters, can contribute to it. These chemicals are used in industry, agriculture, and household products, and when they seep into ground-water, they can infiltrate private wells and public sources of water, silently spreading through the environment.

In this chapter, you'll see how GIS was used to link land-use and environmental data to population and disease data, helping scientists understand how pollution on Cape Cod might be contributing to the region's high rate of breast cancer.

In 1993, the Massachusetts Department of Public Health released cancer data collected throughout the state between 1982 and 1990, showing that the incidence of breast cancer was up to 130 times higher on Cape Cod, a peninsula on the Massachusetts coast, than in other areas of the state.

Since the cape's population resembles that of the rest of the state, researchers speculated that the high rate might be caused by endocrine disrupters found in samples of the cape's soil and ground-water. Unlike natural hormones, which circulate in the blood stream and are metabolized naturally, some endocrine disrupters are not readily broken down and can be stored in fat, remaining in the body for years.

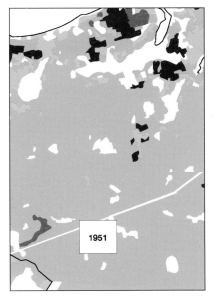
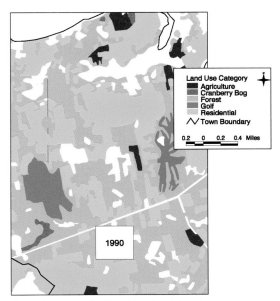

Over the years, homes have been built on Cape Cod's former agricultural land and forests.

Pieces of the puzzle

The department initially awarded a three-year contract to Silent Spring Institute, a nonprofit organization dedicated to studying links between the environment and women's health.

The institute's project team included Applied Geographics, Inc. (AGI, a GIS consultant), Boston University School of Public Health, the Slone Epidemiology Unit of the Boston University School of Medicine, and Tufts University Medical School.

So that researchers could use GIS to enter and manipulate the project data, AGI installed ArcInfo™ and ArcView GIS software at Silent Spring's headquarters. The project data included parcel information from the Cape Cod Commission, the town of Barnstable, and MassGIS at the Executive Office of Environmental Affairs, as well as data on private wells, pollution discharge sites, underground storage tanks, hazardous waste sites, and water distribution pipes and plumes (showing how groundwater conveys contaminants underground). With this data, researchers created maps of the cape's environmental data about such things as water sources, land use, and contaminants.

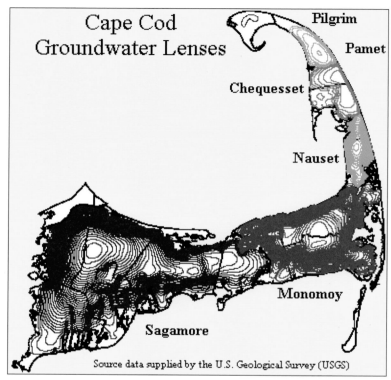

The cape aquifer is divided into six lenses by areas of low groundwater elevation.

Chemical connection

Pesticides had been widely used on Cape Cod for many years. Many pesticides break down very slowly, and are probably still in the cape's soil today.

The team located and compiled pesticide data covering 1940–1990. They tried to include the area sprayed, the years sprayed, and the pesticide's active ingredient. Other data, like the location of former cranberry bogs where pesticides would have been sprayed, was recreated using land-use maps for 1951, 1971, 1984, and 1990 developed by the University of Massachusetts from aerial photographs. Some of these former bogs are now wetlands, while others are the site of housing or industry.

It was also important to divide the bogs into three categories, according to when pesticides would have been applied. Those existing in the 1950s would have been sprayed with DDT, while those existing in the late 1960s might have been sprayed with Sevin.

The GIS was used to show the locations of the chemicals, and when they were applied, for each town on the cape.

On the map below of Falmouth, a purple triangle at the right, along the town border, indicates the extent of an area sprayed with Sevin. This spraying would probably have affected the adjacent town. One of the researchers' chief objectives was to determine how the contamination traveled by aerial drift or through groundwater to affect adjacent areas.

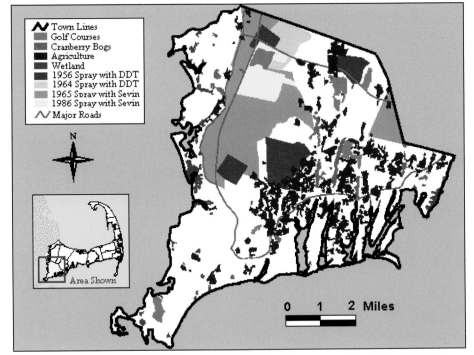

Since pesticides like DDT, used on cranberry bogs and golf courses, are thought to be linked to cancer, the researchers developed pesticide maps to show where chemicals were applied to the area and when.

Seeing the effect

To look at how these pesticides might have polluted the soil and moved through the groundwater, the analysts combined the pollution data with data about the cape's aquifer.

Public water suppliers are in charge of supplying residents with safe drinking water. They are required to estimate the area, or zone, of contribution to a well and any point sources of pollution within this zone. Point sources may include storm drains, discharge pipes, or septic systems, for example. Combining this data let the researchers see which wells might be contaminated by point sources.

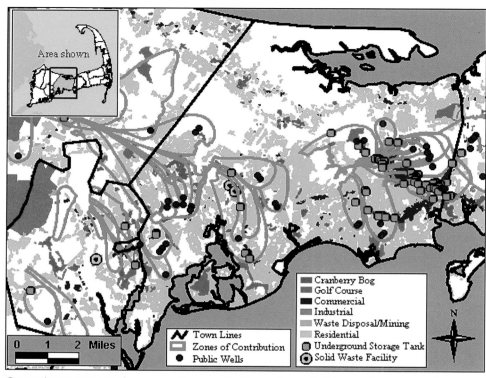

Contaminants may not always come from a patient's own town. As this map shows, areas of contribution (blue lines) often cross over town boundaries (black lines).

Adding patient info

Once they had the environmental data (like cranberry bogs) and the areas of contribution to wells on the same map, researchers were ready to explore the relationship of these locations with the locations of the cape's breast cancer victims.

The team received the addresses of breast cancer patients in January 1996. After eliminating duplicate addresses and the patients who were diagnosed at Cape Cod hospitals but lived somewhere else, they ended up with 2,205 cancer patients who lived on the cape. This information was saved as a dBASE IV™ file and brought into the GIS. All data was kept confidential.

In ArcInfo, AGI created a table with a field for patients' addresses. The table was then divided into 15 tables, one for each of the cape's 15 towns. AGI considered the advantages of address matching using the centerline data versus using the parcel coverage. AGI conducted a pilot test of the data with two towns and found that it could only achieve a 52-percent match rate using the centerline database. So it used the parcel data, which yielded an 85- to 100-percent match rate using the parcel data.

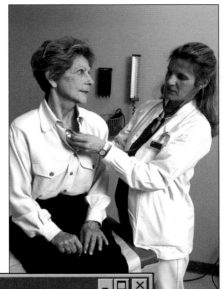

Shape	Id	Patient ID	Address	Street Name	Street Type	Zip Code
Point	1	554341958	12325	Chestnut	Ave	02601
Point	2	439581902	8475	Amber	Way	02563
Point	3	184938274	27342	Matron	St	02644
Point	4	984756327	44564	Dutch	Blvd	02601
Point	5	887384726	845	Killiwetch	Dr	02532
Point	6	663746289	1214	Johannesburg	Dr	02601
Point	7	443982746	18273	Edinger	Way	02563
Point	8	553746182	20734	Oxnard	St	02532
Point	9	982736452	1414	Ellis	Dr	02644
Point	10	207462736	134	Ridgeway	St	02622
Point	11	773645263	24245	View Park	Dr	02563

BC Patient Data

The addresses at the time of diagnosis for more than two thousand breast cancer patients were added to the GIS so researchers could study individual neighborhoods. (The data displayed in this table is fictional and has been created for illustrative purposes only.)

Exposure zones

Now the researchers could use the GIS to assess risk to people living in the towns. They used ArcInfo to calculate the distance from the residential parcels to the likely sources of pollution.

Since forests reduce drift from aerial spraying of pesticides by capturing some of the spray in their foliage, researchers then overlaid data about land use with data about sources of pollution to see where forests came between pollution and homes. They used ArcView GIS to identify the areas with the greatest risk of exposure by selecting residential land-use polygons that intersected or were adjacent to pesticide sources.

This analysis allowed researchers to examine the likelihood that breast cancer victims contracted the disease as a result of being exposed to a point-source pollutant like DDT spray.

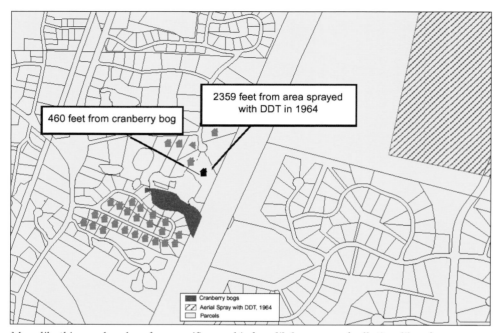

Maps like this one show how far a specific parcel is from likely sources of pollution, like a former cranberry bog and an area sprayed with DDT.

Exposure at home

Maps could now be created for every
town on the cape, showing where pollut-
ants and parcels were. These maps identify parcels, show how far they are from
the nearest source of pesticide, and show
where forests protect them from pollution.

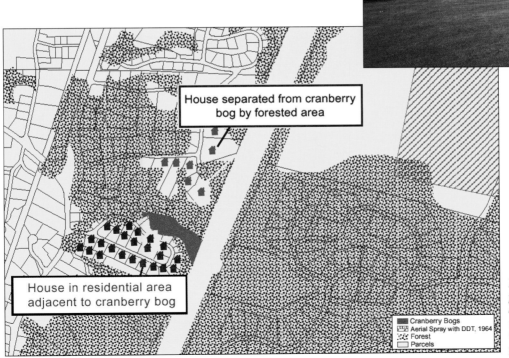

House separated from cranberry
bog by forested area

House in residential area
adjacent to cranberry bog

■ Cranberry Bogs
▨ Aerial Spray with DDT, 1964
▩ Forest
▢ Parcels

*People who live in houses
protected by forest (green)
are thought to be less likely
to get cancer than those
who live right next to a
pollutant (blue).*

Breaking it down

Prior to geocoding the addresses, the researchers only knew how many women had been diagnosed in a town, but not exactly where they lived. With the geocoded data, they could explore the relationship of breast cancer and environmental pollution in much finer detail. They were able to use the GIS to estimate populations for census tracts

and block groups and view that information along with the addresses of women with breast cancer. This allowed them to adjust for differences in age distributions and study incidence in small geographic units that may cross town lines but have similar point sources of pollution. They also used the GIS to see if more people had breast cancer in census block groups

with certain environmental characteristics, such as being adjacent to a former cranberry bog.

Some of these maps have been posted on the Internet at www.silentspring.org/atlas/atlas.htm. At this Web site, visitors can see the statistics for cancer by town, census tract, or census block group.

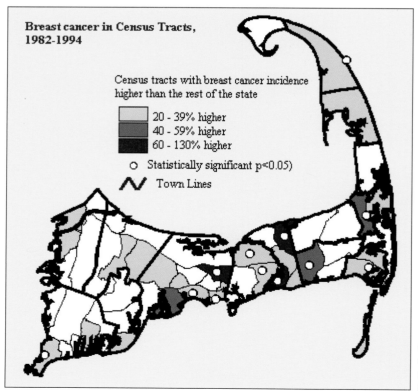

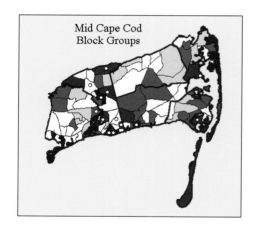

Using the GIS, the team was able to break down the state's cancer incidence data to the census tract and block group levels.

Moving forward

The team will next interview women on Cape Cod, both with breast cancer and without, to find out how long they have lived where they are now and where they lived before that. They will also ask these women questions about family and medical histories, as well as questions about any possible toxic exposures in the workplace and at home. Data from these interviews will be combined with environmental data in the GIS.

Using GIS has permitted the researchers to deal with the data in a way they couldn't previously, conducting "what-if" studies on individual houses and towns. By applying the latest GIS technology to public health research, the team hopes to identify previously unstudied, preventable causes of the disease.

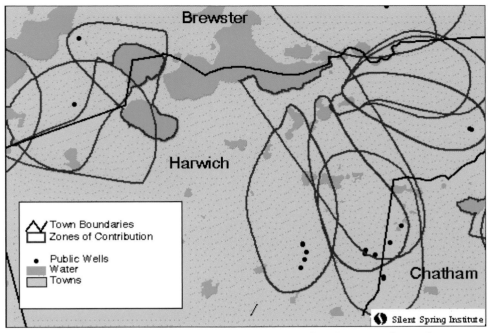

The GIS that Silent Spring Institute and AGI created during the first three years of research represents the most comprehensive source of information on the Cape Cod environment.

The system

Hardware: Sun® SPARC™ 20, Apple® Macintosh® computers

Software: ArcInfo, ArcView GIS, ArcPress™

The data

Cancer, parcel, infrastructure, hydrological and well, and land-use data

The people

Special thanks to Joan Gardner, president of Applied Geographics, Inc., to Silent Spring Institute, and to the Massachusetts Department of Public Health.

Chapter 4

•••••• Breaking the cycle

NOT ALL SUCCESS STORIES are success stories. Some are only partial victories—victories, such as they are, torn roughly from impossible circumstances. One such partial victory is that over malaria. Malaria is caused by a microorganism carried by the Anopheles mosquito. For most residents of the Northern Hemisphere, a mosquito bite is no more than a minor annoyance. But, in portions of East Africa, especially Kenya, malaria kills between 1.5 and 2.7 million people a year, most of them during the six-month rainy season. More than 50 percent are children less than five years old who have not yet developed immunity to the disease.

In this chapter, you'll see how the Division of Parasitic Diseases of the Centers for Disease Control and Prevention (CDC) in Atlanta, Georgia, uses ArcView GIS software in western Kenya to help its malaria research.

Nine out of ten malaria cases throughout the world occur in Africa. The country of Kenya has been especially hard hit.

In Kenya, the CDC works with the Kenya Medical Research Institute to study malaria and to work to prevent it. Nearly three hundred researchers work on various projects near Lake Victoria and Kisumu, Kenya's third largest town. These researchers use Differential Global Positioning Systems (DGPS) to collect positions and data in the field, and then edit and analyze this data in ArcView GIS.

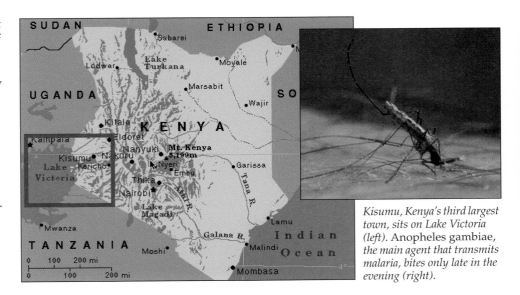

Kisumu, Kenya's third largest town, sits on Lake Victoria (left). Anopheles gambiae, the main agent that transmits malaria, bites only late in the evening (right).

Fighting the resistance

The rapid resurgence of malaria and other vector-borne diseases in Africa comes in part from the resistance that has developed to many classes of antimicrobial drugs and insecticides. Many researchers are working on different vaccines, but this solution is still years away.

With effective antimalarial drugs costing too much for most Africans and with their effectiveness declining, the research team had to look for other ways to combat the problem. With the newest technology wavering, researchers looked back in time for answers.

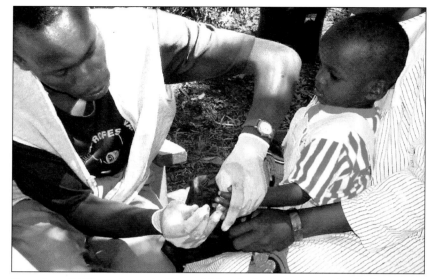

Every hour, 1,500 people, most of them children in developing countries, die from one of six infectious diseases: tuberculosis, malaria, measles, chronic diarrhea, AIDS, and acute respiratory diseases (like pneumonia and flu). Of these, malaria is the only insect-borne parasitic disease.

Old method, new twist

Untreated bednets have long been used
in the tropics as a way to prevent insect-
borne diseases. Although they can be
free-standing, most of these finely woven
nets hang from the ceiling and are used to
cover people at night, when the Anopheles mosquito feeds.

Most bednets today are treated with
odorless insecticides, which offer even
better protection. Treated bednets not
only prevent mosquitoes from getting too
close, but also repel them. But to be effective, bednets, which cost about five dollars each, must be well maintained and
used properly.

Researchers at the CDC set out to see if
this age-old method could have modern-
day success.

*Every six months, the
bednets must be dipped in
insecticide and thoroughly
dried before use. (The photo
at the left is reproduced with
the permission of Canada's
International Development
Research Centre and the
World Health Organization.
Photographer: A. Haaland.)*

Maps from points

To conduct the bednet study, the CDC chose an area known for its high incidence of malaria. The last map of the study region was made in the late 1960s, so researchers began by creating an updated map of the 225-square-mile region just outside of Kisumu along Lake Victoria.

Mapping this region proved to be a momentous task. The DGPS mapping team hired local fisherman to row them in small fishing boats to map the shore of the lake. Roads were mapped by driving cars along them while a team member captured location data with the DGPS.

Once they had an updated map of the region, they could begin creating the maps that would help them understand the impact of bednets on malaria, childhood mortality, and mosquito populations.

Members of the CDC-led Bednet team that conducts malaria surveillance, distributes bednets, and monitors their use in the study area.

Local fishermen helped the GPS team map the shore of Lake Victoria.

Setting the stage

Before a large-scale study can be performed, researchers must understand the factors affecting malaria transmission, mosquito abundance, and childhood mortality in the study area.

GIS played an important role in this process. Researchers used it to compute spatial variables that play an important role in statistical models predicting mosquito abundance and other factors affecting malaria transmission.

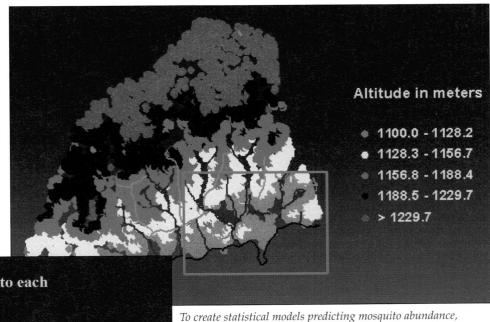

Altitude in meters

- 1100.0 - 1128.2
- 1128.3 - 1156.7
- 1156.8 - 1188.4
- 1188.5 - 1229.7
- > 1229.7

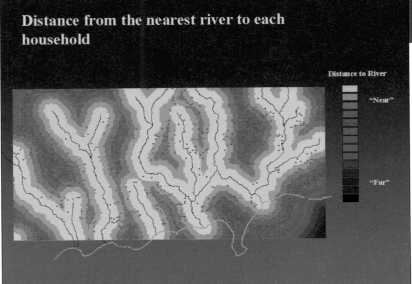

Distance from the nearest river to each household

Distance to River

"Near"

"Far"

To create statistical models predicting mosquito abundance, researchers used maps to study features such as altitude, and GIS to compute important variables such as distance to the nearest river.

Catch them if you can

Prior to the bednet study, researchers had been trapping mosquitoes and studying malaria in children in a 15-village subset of the bednet study area. The monthly maps helped the researchers understand the results of statistical models predicting mosquito prevalence. The surface maps helped them find "hot spots" and see how they grew during the rainy season and contracted during the dry season.

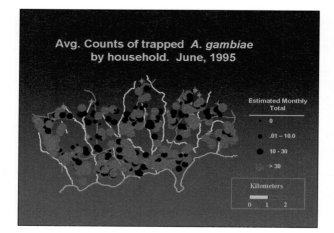

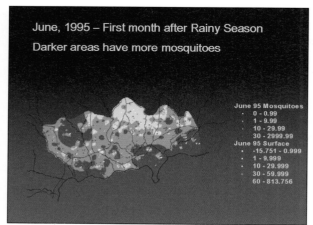

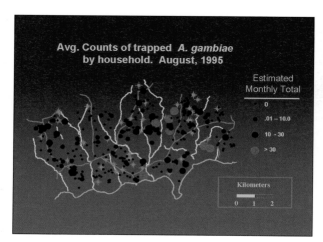

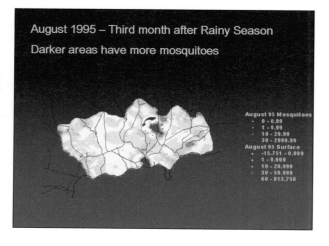

These views of the 15-village study area show the number of mosquitoes trapped in homes during rainy (June) and dry (August) months. The darker areas in the surface maps are the mosquito "hot spots" for that month.

Tracking deaths to save lives

CDC researchers were not sure if the bednets would be effective in an area where
many people receive more than one hundred bites in a year. Even if the nets pre-
vented 90 percent of all bites, there was
considerable doubt that this would be
enough to have an impact on mortality.

This careful study before the nets were
distributed allowed the CDC to divide
the study area into two parts that were
roughly equal with respect to childhood
mortality, mosquito abundance, and
malaria transmission.

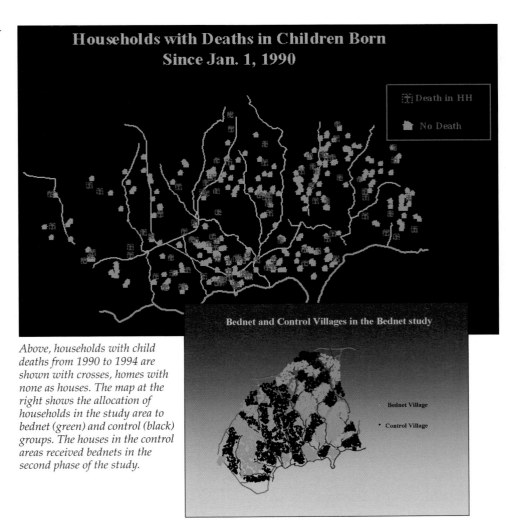

*Above, households with child
deaths from 1990 to 1994 are
shown with crosses, homes with
none as houses. The map at the
right shows the allocation of
households in the study area to
bednet (green) and control (black)
groups. The houses in the control
areas received bednets in the
second phase of the study.*

Bringing help home

Early results indicate that the bednets have been surprisingly effective in reducing morbidity and mortality in children.

One promising approach involves moving the production and treatment of the nets to the local area. More research has begun on making the nets more affordable and easier to use. A new insecticide being evaluated costs one-tenth as much and lasts twice as long. The feasibility of local net production is being studied. Not only would this reduce costs, but it would stimulate the economy by providing jobs.

With children most at risk, and an economy in desperate need of help, moving bednet production to the local villages seems to offer the best hope for success.

The system

Hardware: 75 PCs connected in a local area network; Trimble DGPS units; Magellan ProMark X GPS units

Software: ArcView GIS, ArcView Spatial Analyst

The data

Field data includes DGPS geographic features (roads, houses, schools, hospitals, rivers, and shorelines), demographics, epidemiology, and historical data on deaths, sicknesses, and mosquito abundance.

The people

Special thanks to Allen W. Hightower of the CDC's Division of Parasitic Diseases.

DPD
DIVISION OF
PARASITIC
DISEASES
NCID / CDC

Chapter 5

Making the right calls

DOCTORS ARE IN THE BUSINESS OF HEALING PEOPLE. The companies that supply patients with drugs, however, are in the business of developing and marketing new advances in medicine and educating doctors in the use of these therapies. As new drugs become available, pharmaceutical companies have to compete on the open market like any other company, spending thousands, sometimes millions, of dollars promoting their products and sending field representatives with samples and literature into hospitals and physicians' offices.

In the past few years, with the advent of physician-specific prescription data, this sales method has been finely tuned, with the companies preparing reps with data about each physician's prescription-writing habits and how many sales calls to make to each office each year.

In this chapter, you'll see how Health Products Research (HPR) , based in Whitehouse, New Jersey, uses GIS to map call locations and balance the representatives' sales territories.

Health Products Research, a division of Ventiv Health, Inc., analyzes sales territories for almost a third of the world's pharmaceutical companies.

Typically, sales territories are assigned by ZIP Code boundaries, or occasionally by county lines or even national borders, rather than by the volume of customers in an area. Areas defined strictly by geographic boundaries often produce uneven results, with some salespeople being assigned more accounts than they can handle, and others receiving fewer than their fair share. Without a way to view the workload data geographically, HPR's clients were at a loss to know how to divide the accounts equitably.

Health Products Research, based in Whitehouse, New Jersey, leads the industry in designing sales territories for pharmaceutical and health care companies.

GIS to the rescue

HPR begins by collecting data about all prescriptions written in the past 12 to 24 months by each physician in the United States, including the number of prescriptions written each month and the brands prescribed.

HPR's Strategic Resource Allocation Group then can see which physicians are most likely to write prescriptions for a particular product. A statistical analysis of this data using modeling software helps them determine the optimum number of calls that need to be made to each doctor. For example, modeling establishes that calling 12 times on Dr. Smith, who frequently prescribes drugs similar to the new product, will yield $150 per call, while the thirteenth call will only yield $90. Since sending the rep out costs the company $100, the model only allocates 12 calls to that doctor.

The results of this analysis, displayed at the right, show that for this group of physicians, fewer than six calls will result in loss of market share, while more than twelve calls will yield very little increase in share.

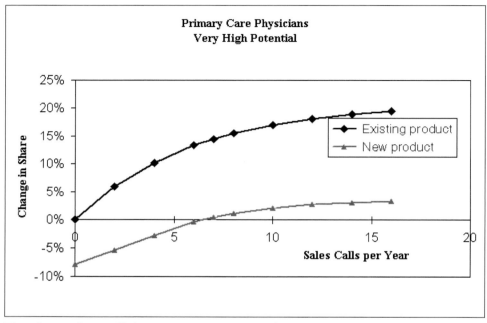

These doctors, the most likely ones to write prescriptions for the new product, will still require six to twelve visits from the sales representative.

Bringing geography into the equation

Now that the company knows how many calls to make to each physician, it needs to give this information a geographic context. To do this, the analysts use statistical software to sum up how many calls will have to be made to physicians in each ZIP Code. Being able to see the call numbers distributed on a map helps the companies divide the sales territories by workload so that each rep handles about the same number of calls.

HPR then brings the database results into PharmAlign Desktop, a GIS application written using ArcView GIS software, which allows them to create maps so clients can see the results of the realignment study for themselves.

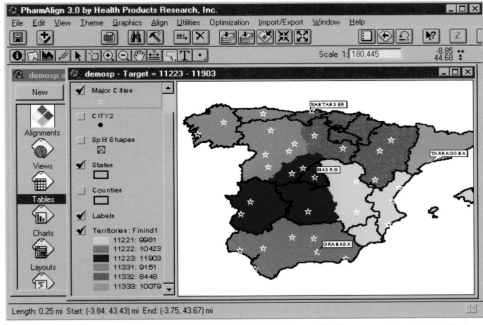

This map shows the numerical balance (number of sales calls) graphically among the sales territories.

Aligning territories

The number of calls for each territory can now be balanced with the ArcView GIS database tools.

In this study, the "before" workloads ranged from 850 calls to 1,150 calls for each rep and they were crossing paths in some areas.

Using PharmAlign Desktop, the analysts redistributed the calls, giving each about 1,000 calls to balance the workload. The realignment is illustrated here.

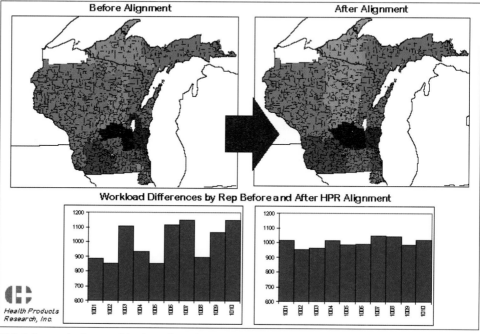

This before-and-after graphic shows how the realignment produces better geographic balance of the reps' territories. The bar charts show that the number of calls are now all within about 10 percent of each other, an equitable workload distribution.

Map making in the field

HPR provides customized color maps to its clients. The maps are a valuable tool, used by field management to assess sales opportunities and to orient new sales reps. The maps are created using ESRI's MapObjects software.

The GIS files required to produce the maps also can be provided to field management via PharmAlign Field Manager, a PC-based software product developed by HPR for its clients. This tool helps field management view market information in a geographic format. The data can identify areas of opportunity as well as areas requiring an adjustment in workload.

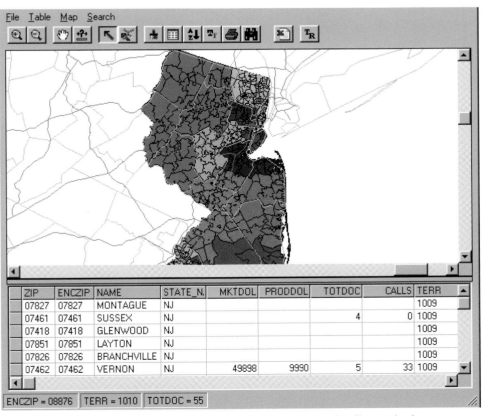

PharmAlign Field Manager allows the sales manager to easily view and realign territories.

Making the case

Ventiv Health U.S. Sales, a sister division of HPR, uses PharmAlign to present marketplace data to potential clients, hoping to convince them to hire Ventiv's sales forces to boost sales of a pharmaceutical product.

They follow a similar process of collecting and analyzing physician prescription-writing data, but look for pockets of opportunity—where the physicians most likely to prescribe the drug are located—and offer to make calls to those locations on a contract basis.

The ability to show prospective clients the results of an analysis as charts and maps often gives Ventiv the edge over its competition in landing these accounts.

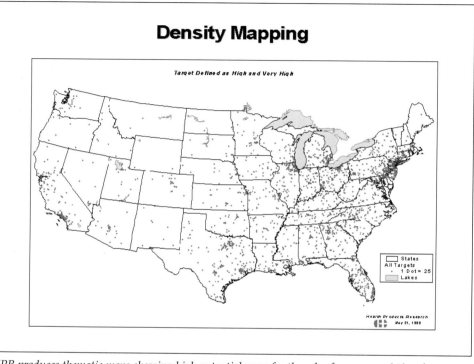

HPR produces thematic maps showing high-potential areas for the sale of a new or existing drug.

Adding to the bottom line

HPR plans to make improvements to PharmAlign Desktop so the software can be used by more clients—smaller pharmaceutical organizations and companies in other branches of the health care field that also use sales reps.

HPR is also improving PharmAlign Desktop and Field Manager so that district managers will be able to "live link" over the Internet to HPR's physician-level databases to allow up-to-date refreshes of maps and data.

Ventiv Health is expanding the use of GIS in its divisions and for its customers, so that they can link into the company's data over the Internet and update their sales territory maps.

The system

Hardware: PCs (Pentium® II or better)

Software: ArcView GIS, MapObjects

The data

Customer-specific geographic and physician-level data on prescriptions and detailing activity.

The people

Special thanks to the Sales Force Deployment and Analysis department at Health Products Research.

Health Products Research
INC.

A DIVISION OF VENTIV|
|HEALTH

Chapter 6

•••••• Comparing apples to apples

TWO 50-YEAR-OLD PATIENTS IN WISCONSIN, one in Milwaukee and the other in Madison, have similar heart conditions and overall health. Yet, statistics predict they'll receive different treatments. Why? Because each local health care market in the United States is unique, with unique hospitals and unique doctors with specialized skills. Statistics about differences in resources (hospital beds, physicians, and spending) and how they're used (hospitalizations, surgical procedures, and care for the terminally ill) are published in *The Dartmouth Atlas of Health Care in the United States.*

In 1998, the atlas was published for the first time on CD–ROM. Called the Dartmouth Atlas Data Viewer, this version includes GIS software to help physicians, researchers, HMOs, and statisticians query and visualize how local resources are distributed and compare health care practices in their own area with those in other areas.

In this chapter, you'll see how a group of business coalitions is using the data viewer to create maps, diagrams, and charts that help members, like General Motors Corporation, understand how doctors apply a single set of health benefits in 14 different plant locations across the country.

The Midwest Business Group on Health (MBGH) is a business coalition that helps members evaluate local health care markets. The group has traditionally used *The Dartmouth Atlas of Health Care in the United States* for these analyses, but recently started using the data viewer, a CD–ROM version of the atlas that includes ArcView GIS software for querying and viewing the data and for creating maps and charts.

To encourage its members to use the data viewer, MBGH teamed with the American Hospital Association's Health Research and Educational Trust. Funded by the Robert Wood Johnson Foundation, the project explored the variations in treatments and costs in three health care markets, where two coalitions (Kansas Employer Coalition on Health and The Greater Milwaukee Business Group on Health) and an employer member (General Motors Corporation) are located. MBGH showed them how to use the viewer to analyze data about their local markets and help the project's analysts make appropriate comparisons.

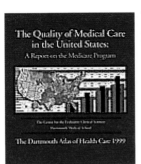

The Dartmouth Atlas of Health Care in the United States *provides an overview of the nation's health care resources and delivery.*

Small-area analysis

The statistics in the data viewer are for analyzing small areas or for looking at local health care statistics to see how services are used by defined populations.

The viewer's 3,436 Hospital Service Areas (HSAs) describe an area where people seek immediate care from that hospital. Hospital Referral Regions (HRRs) indicate a service area for referral or specialty care and can encompass several HSAs. The viewer has 306 HRRs.

For a comparison of local markets, the analysts select a region and viewing level by clicking on HRR or HSA. This opening map shows HRRs in the Midwest (by color). HSAs have also been selected but are not displayed at this scale.

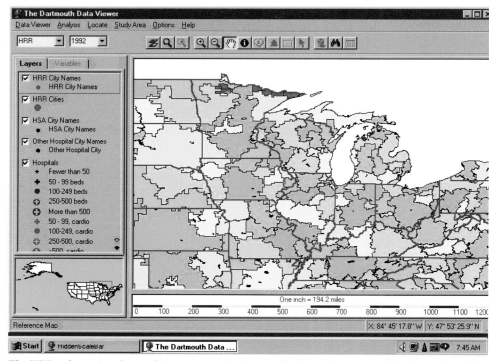

The HRRs, shown in color on this map, are referral areas. Patients often cross political boundaries like state lines to visit referral facilities for specialty care.

Treatment profiles

The analysts select Milwaukee and Madison for the first comparison. By clicking on the Milwaukee area, they can zoom in to study it in more detail. At this scale, city names and symbols indicating hospital size can be displayed.

The analysts want to see how the costs for treatments vary by geographic area. This data will help them develop "treatment profiles" at the HRR level. Treatment profiles describe how often certain treatments or procedures are performed in comparable populations.

Because heart disease is one of the most common causes of death in the United States, the analysts decide to look at cardiac surgery first. In some regions, doctors perform more bypass grafts, which is an expensive treatment, but in other areas, doctors seem to prefer balloon angioplasty, which costs much less. The analysts query the viewer for data on these procedures (per one thousand patients) in both Milwaukee and Madison, using a color ramp to show the percentage of bypass grafts for each HRR. Madison is directly west of Milwaukee, but the treatment for cardiac patients is less costly.

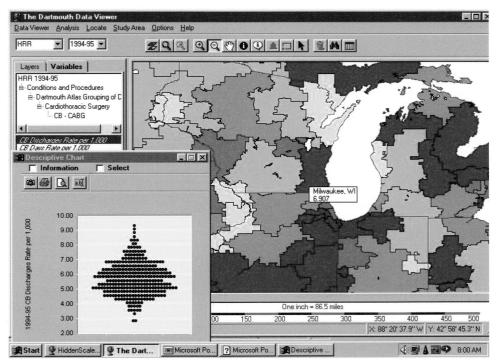

The darker the HRR, the more likely that a cardiac patient there will undergo a bypass graft.

Milwaukee vs. Madison

The analysts can view data about treatments like cardiac bypass grafts and balloon angioplasty as distribution diagrams, which show them how individual HSAs or HRRs compare for these treatments.

The distribution diagram at the left shows the cardiac bypass percentages. Each purple dot is an HRR shown on the map of the Midwest from the previous page. Milwaukee, with a cardiac bypass rate of 6.907, is the yellow dot on the chart's right nearest the top. For comparison, the HRRs of Muncie and Topeka are also highlighted in yellow. These are regions where the companies involved in this study are located and where their employees would seek care.

From this diagram, the analysts see that bypass grafts are performed more often in the Milwaukee HRR than in the other two areas. The distribution diagram at the right shows the percentages for balloon angioplasty, the less costly treatment. On this diagram, the yellow dots again indicate Milwaukee, Muncie, and Topeka.

Milwaukee is the lowest dot on this diagram, with fewer than six patients per thousand undergoing this treatment.

Both the map and distribution diagrams can be shown on the screen at the same time so the analysts can select a dot on the diagram and highlight the region on the map, or vice versa.

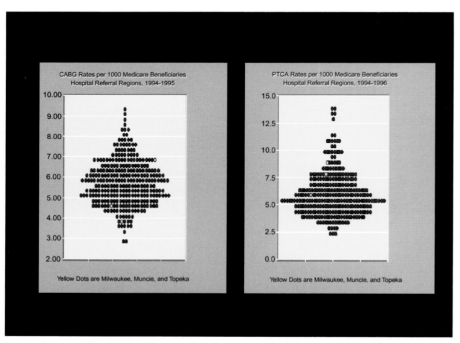

The analysts use distribution diagrams like these, a standard chart available in the viewer, to compare data another way. On these charts, the selected HRRs (yellow dots) are shown in comparison with the other HRRs in the Midwest (purple dots) for two types of heart surgeries.

Charting the data

Since the purpose of this project is to test the usefulness of the viewer's different analysis tools for MBGH's members, the analysts next create a benchmark chart, which is another way to display the statistical data for comparison.

This chart allows them to display data, like procedure rates for HRRs or HSAs in their study as compared to other HRRs or HSAs, to national averages, or to a managed care organization norm.

They select six HRRs for the chart (highlighted in yellow on the map) and four procedures, two cardiac procedures (CB and PTCA), a bypass surgery of the prostate gland (PT), and back surgery (BS). These are compared with national averages.

On the benchmark chart, HRRs with rates for these procedures higher than the national average are shown to the right of the centerline; those with lower rates are to the left.

Using this chart, the analysts can show the participating companies how their regions stack up to the national averages for these procedures, and their health care specialists can get an idea of how costs vary in the different markets.

The analysts will use the viewer to look at rates for other surgeries and to evaluate the availability of resources, like how many cardiovascular specialists are in certain areas.

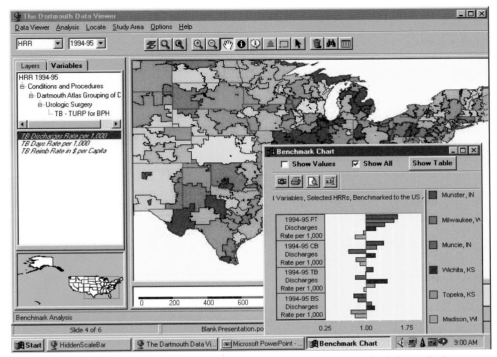

Benchmark charts help analysts understand the excess or deficit of resources in their results in comparison to regional averages, national averages, or any other benchmark.

Applying the data

Before turning the examples over to the companies, the analysts add hospitalization data to a chart of the four procedures. The chart benchmarks this data to national averages so the analysts can see where patients were hospitalized more or less often for the same conditions. For prostate surgery at Munster, for example, the index is 1.59, or 60 percent higher than the national average, while Madison is 20 percent lower.

For large companies, like the members of MBGH, knowing the hospitalization data in different markets and how it compares with national averages is useful when determining the quality of care health care providers will offer employees. These comparisons are not just about where resources are located, but how they're used, which is much more meaningful information for companies buying health coverage for employees.

The maps and charts prepared by the analysts were presented to the members, many of whom have said they'll use the viewer and its powerful analysis and data-viewing tools for future market studies.

More information about how the data was used is in a free publication, *A Health Care Purchaser's Guide to Using the Dartmouth Atlas*, available from MBGH. See www.mbgh.org for more information.

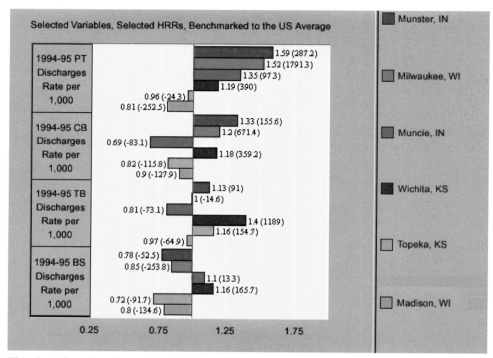

This chart shows how frequently people are hospitalized for these procedures relative to the national averages.

The system

Hardware: PC

Software: *The Dartmouth Atlas of Health Care in the United States,* which includes ArcView GIS software

The data

All data for this project is included on the Dartmouth Atlas Data Viewer CD–ROM.

The people

Special thanks to Tom Granatir, director of quality initiatives for the American Hospital Association, and James D. Mortimer, president of the Midwest Business Group on Health.

Chapter 7

•••••• Mapping a niche

SOONER OR LATER IT HAPPENS TO US ALL—laugh lines slightly deeper than yesterday, colds that last a week instead of a day, strands of silver among the gold. Right now more people are approaching the "golden years" than ever before, and they need the health care industry to keep up with their growing numbers. Already a number of options exist in addition to the traditional nursing homes: assisted-living centers, in-home care services, and physician-directed fitness centers. But they need even more.

In this chapter, you'll see how Project Market Decisions, Inc. (PMD), a market research/market feasibility firm, uses GIS to aid one such company, GerAssist, in siting locations for new assisted-living centers in Nashville.

Covering Florida, South Carolina, and Tennessee, GerAssist, Inc., of Brentwood, Tennessee, offers a number of interesting variations on the nursing home theme. You can live at home and have nurses drop by when you need them, or have nurses who stay there with you round the clock. You can move to an apartment with nurses on duty all the time. You can even go to fitness centers run by doctors.

GerAssist used GIS services from PMD to decide where in Tennessee to build more assisted-living centers.

In assisted-living communities, seniors get help with daily activities such as cooking, cleaning, and transportation.

Where they live...

The company knows that people who decide to move into an assisted-living community prefer to stay close to home, within a five- to ten-minute drive so that surroundings are familiar, or only as far as the distance to an adult child's residence.

The typical resident of these centers is over 75, with an annual income of at least $18,800, so PMD used census data sorted by age and income to find out where people like that currently live. This data was brought into ArcView GIS and displayed by graduated color.

From the map, the analysts could see that many people over 75 with a sufficient income live in the suburban areas surrounding Nashville, especially in two ZIP Codes south of the city.

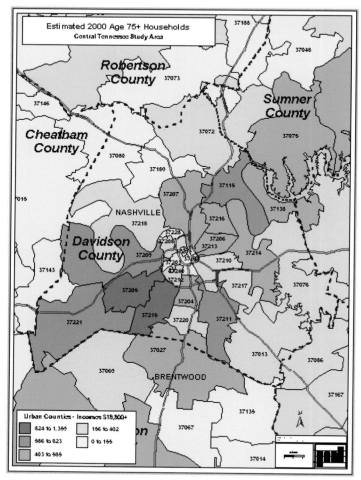

Bright green and green mark ZIP Codes where many people live who are over 75 and have an income of $18,800 a year or more.

...and need to stay

PMD's analysts then used the census data to create a map showing where people live who were likely to have parents over the age of 75. They used ArcView GIS to select and display ZIP Codes with large percentages of middle-aged (45 to 64), high-income (over $75,000) households.

These people also live mainly to the south of the city. Facilities located in this area would indeed be conveniently located.

But not all seniors will need care as they get older, and some of those who do will choose to receive it in their own homes or with family members. Only about 14 percent of 75-and-up seniors with a minimum annual income of $18,800 will choose to move to an assisted-living center.

So PMD used the ArcView GIS Map Calculator to adjust and display the demand for assisted-living facilities in each ZIP Code.

The number of adult children also had to be adjusted since not all middle-aged people have living parents, and of those who do, not all will move their parents close by.

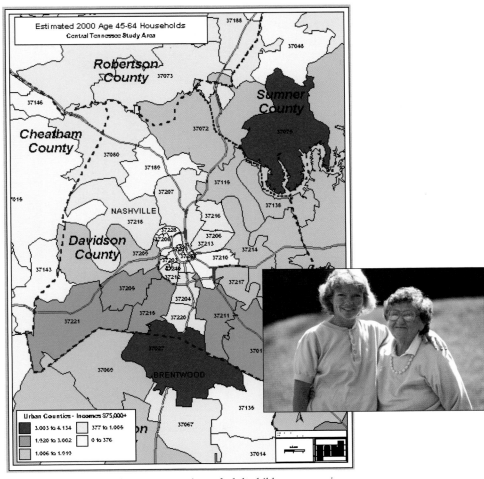

Dark blue shows the highest concentrations of adult children or caregivers of the center's target population.

Where there's no competition

Now that they knew where all the likely candidates lived, they had to find out where assisted-living centers already were, or where other companies were planning to open some.

Analysts brought state data about the competition, along with PMD's proprietary database, into ArcView GIS and viewed it as a table. Included in the table were names of the facilities, their addresses, and how many beds they had. The analysts used a script, created by PMD with the Avenue™ programming language for ArcView GIS, to draw a market area around each facility based on population density. The script then allocated the beds from the facilities to the ZIP Codes comprising each facility's market area. When they overlaid this data with that showing the demand for these services, they could see where the demand was not being met.

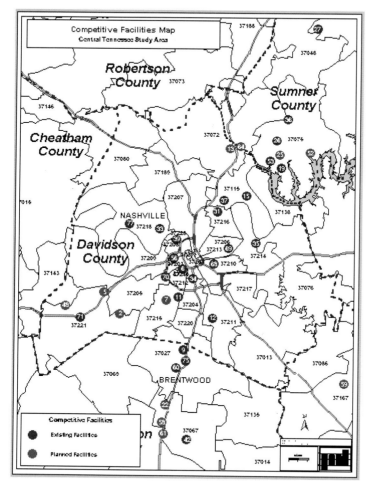

Several assisted-living facilities are planned (pink) or already exist (blue) in the Nashville area.

Seeing the GAP

Areas where there were qualifying seniors but not enough assisted-living centers became possible locations for new GerAssist facilities. Determining where such gaps exist is called a Geographic Allocation Process (GAP) analysis.

Again PMD used the Map Calculator, this time to subtract the number of available beds from the number of people within each ZIP Code who would need beds. In this way they could see whether an existing center was large enough to accommodate all the qualifying people within its 5-mile radius. A center that's too small may leave a gap to be filled, while a very large center might be able to serve people within a wider radius.

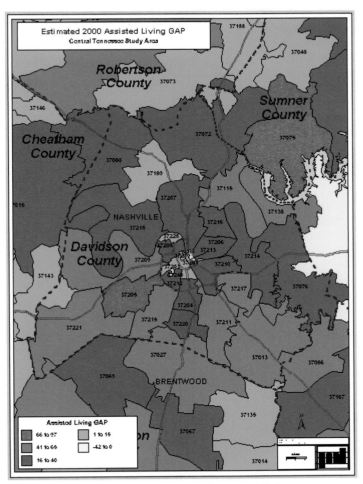

The areas with the highest unmet demand for assisted-living centers are shown in red.

Reaching conclusions

In the final report provided to GerAssist, maps showed the best ZIP Codes in the Nashville area for opening new assisted-living facilities. Analysts could also extrapolate from the same data the best markets for GerAssist's other products and services.

The report also included projections about how each market would change over the next five or ten years.

Already, GerAssist has built two new facilities in Nashville and planned two more.

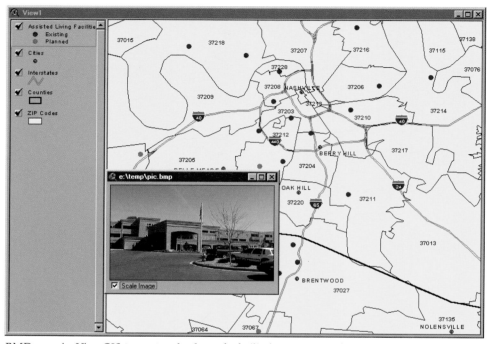

PMD uses ArcView GIS to create a database of a facility's competitors that can include "hotlinked" photos.

The system

Hardware: Dell® PCs

Software: Atlas GIS™ and ArcView GIS

The data

Customer, street, census, and business data

The people

Special thanks to David Shuey, vice president of Data and GIS Services at PMD.

Project Market Decisions
a ZA Consulting company

Turning market data into management decisions®

Chapter 8

Getting back to work

ACCORDING TO THE BUREAU OF LABOR STATISTICS, U.S. Department of Labor, 6.1 million people suffered an injury on the job in 1997. Nearly half of those people lost time at work as a result of their injuries. When workers get injured, employers and health care providers want them treated, healed, and back on the job as soon as possible. When the centers that offer these services are conveniently located, employees also save money and time getting to them.

In this chapter, you'll see how Jewish Hospital HealthCare Services (JHHS) uses ArcView GIS software to tailor its services to the needs of employers by locating specialized rehabilitation centers near them.

A leader in medical care throughout Kentucky and southern Indiana for more than 90 years, Jewish Hospital is known throughout the world as a high-tech specialty center, developing cutting-edge advancements in a full range of medical specialties. With this kind of expertise in all areas, employers know they can trust JHHS to help their employees get better and back to work as soon as possible.

The JHHS network offers its services at 35 locations in this region, including hospitals and outpatient centers. These are doing so well that JHHS will open more of them, but naturally the network must site each new facility carefully—close to its target audience, but without overlapping service areas.

The JHHS network, which serves over 300,000 patients annually, offers rehabilitation for back, neck, head, and limb injuries.

The EmployCare advantage

With services in just about every area of medical expertise, it's no surprise that JHHS operates a comprehensive occupational health program. Called Employ-Care, this program offers a broad range of preventive care and other services far beyond a traditional workers' compensation program, focusing on preventing injuries and maintaining health. Through EmployCare, JHHS provides 24-hour treatment for work-related injuries and illnesses, as well as rehabilitation services, programs teaching health and safety, employment physicals, and employee drug and alcohol screenings. JHHS even offers consulting services, which means they'll come to you to assess the safety of your work environment or to conduct on-site health and safety seminars.

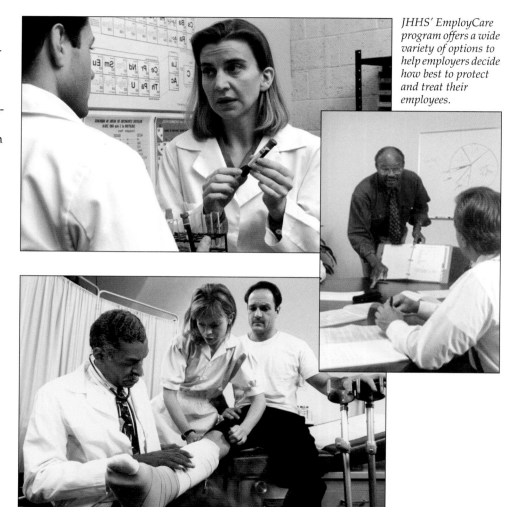

JHHS' EmployCare program offers a wide variety of options to help employers decide how best to protect and treat their employees.

Locating patients

To continue providing the best possible occupational health services as it adds new centers, JHHS must first keep track of where patients and employers are located in relation to existing JHHS facilities.

JHHS operates nine centers in the greater Louisville area. Its Corporate Planning analysts began by mapping these facilities, their service areas, and the addresses of their patients.

First, the analysts imported outpatient data for 1998 into ArcView GIS and geocoded it to create the map at the right showing where patients live (green dots). They then added the locations of clinics (purple dots) and used ArcView GIS to determine each clinic's 3-mile service area.

When deciding where to build another clinic, the analysts can use this data to help determine which locations have enough potential patients but don't overlap another center's service area.

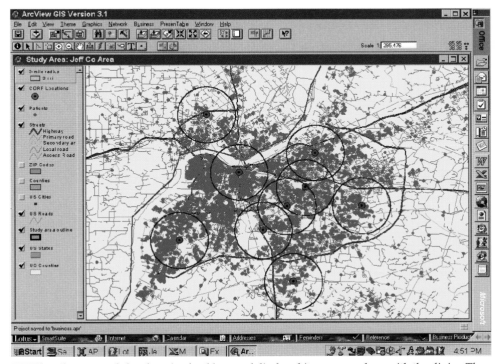

JHHS' analysts geocoded each patient's address and displayed it on a map along with the clinics. The blue circles represent the ideal service area for each clinic.

Making a beeline

Sometimes patients who live within one clinic's service area are not using that clinic. To see where patients were going, JHHS used ArcView GIS to draw lines from each patient's address to the center that patient uses. These lines not only show where patients are receiving treatment, but whether they're crossing over service areas to do so.

From this map, they can see that many patients are, in fact, not driving to the center closest to their home. There can be many reasons for this. For example, some injuries may only be treated at certain locations, or a patient may be getting treatment closer to where they work than where they live.

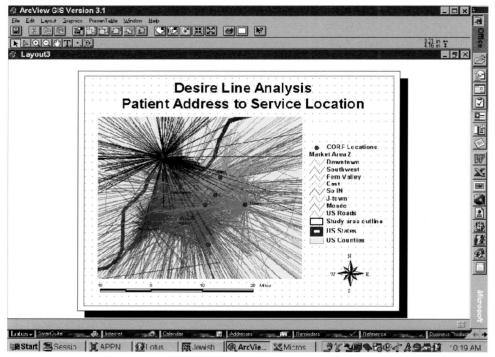

Maps like this one show where a patient goes to receive treatment and whether they are crossing service areas.

Reallocating patients

To find out why some patients are driving farther for treatment, the analysts add more information to their database, including the address for each patient's employer, as well as the type of treatment for which each person has been referred. The analysts then query the database to see which patients are using a center that isn't close to their home or place of work and who don't require more specialized care.

Since there's no obvious reason for these patients to be traveling so far, the analysts use ArcView GIS to reallocate them to clinics closer to home. These patients were often simply unaware of the closer center and usually appreciate being reassigned because it saves them time and money.

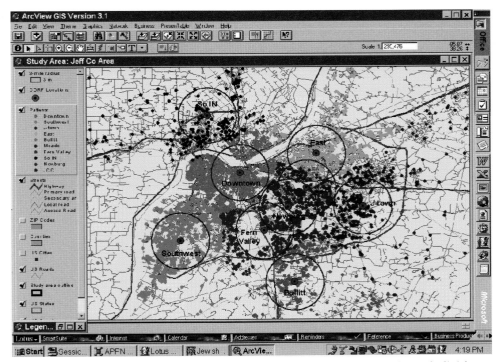

After assigning patients to clinics closer to home, JHHS uses ArcView GIS to display each clinic's patients with a unique color.

Finding employers

When it comes to occupational health, knowing where the employers are is just as important as knowing where patients live.

Although the analysts have added each patient's employer to the database, there may also be employers out there who are unaware of JHHS clinics in their area. Not only do the analysts want to find out where employers are, they also want to determine the injuries employees there are most likely to suffer.

Certain employers have higher injury rates than others, or have employees who suffer specific types of injuries more often. In an industrial area, for example, employers see more back injuries, toxic exposure illnesses, and broken bones. In an office environment, however, stress-related illness and strains from repetitive motion are much more common.

To get a closer look at where each area's employers are, the JHHS analysts use GIS to see whether there are enough centers in these areas or whether the centers that are there offer the right types of services. JHHS can also use this information to more aggressively market its services to employers who may not be aware of the wide range of services offered through the EmployCare program.

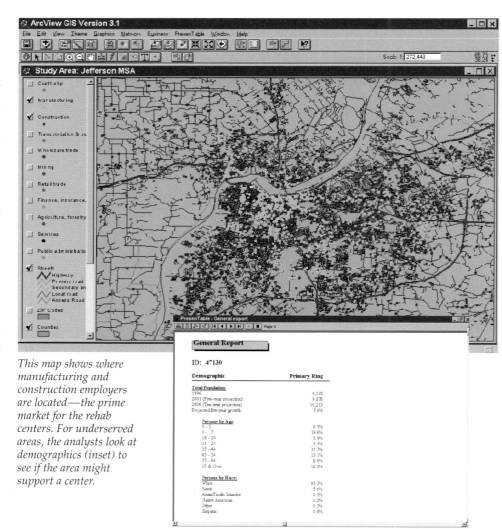

This map shows where manufacturing and construction employers are located—the prime market for the rehab centers. For underserved areas, the analysts look at demographics (inset) to see if the area might support a center.

Help on the Internet

Jewish Hospital HealthCare Services provides information about all of its programs, including EmployCare, on the Internet at www.jhhs.org/index.html. Employers and others can visit this Web site to find out about JHHS programs and services, locate a nearby center, choose a physician, read current news articles about JHHS, and examine new technologies being explored by JHHS' network of world-renowned specialists.

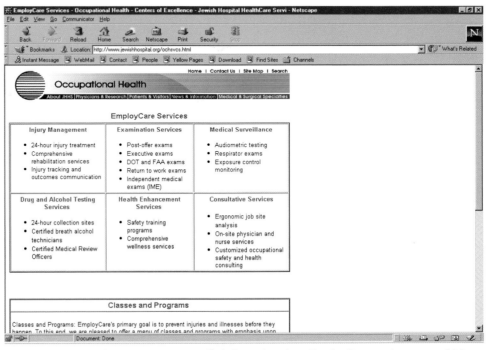

On the Internet, employers can access specific information about EmployCare services to see which ones are right for them.

The system

Hardware: Compaq® 486 laptop running Windows 95

Software: ArcView GIS, ArcView Business Analyst

The data

Demographic, business, and outpatient data

The people

Special thanks to Greg Pugh, corporate planning manager at JHHS.

Chapter 9

Cutting costs

ACCORDING TO WORKERS COMPENSATION LAWS in most states, employers are responsible for medical costs of on-the-job injuries. Tracking these injuries is a daunting task for large and small employers, yet uncovering injury patterns helps employers focus on preventive efforts.

CorVel Corporation uses two GIS products—BodyViewer™ and Patient Access—to help employers understand their employees' most common injuries. BodyViewer determines the most common injuries, the cost of treating these injuries, and the potential savings for the employer. Patient Access determines the accessibility and comprehensiveness of network providers for the injured worker.

CorVel's managed care network increases quality of care while dramatically cutting employer costs. Insurance companies, third-party administrators, and self-administered employers typify customers using CorVel's services. In addition to a preferred provider network of hospitals, specialty physicians, general practitioners, and outpatient clinics, CorVel helps clients review patients' medical bills, workman's compensation claims, and disability services. Clients can use this information to decide if the current benefits package or payment structure is right for them.

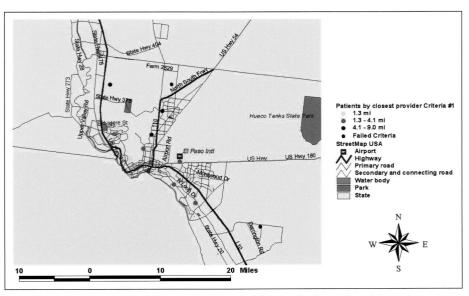

While data is the nature of its business, CorVel uses GIS to make the results of the analyses visual—making statistics easier for clients to interpret and use.

The body view

CorVel uses BodyViewer, an ArcView GIS extension developed by GeoHealth, Inc., of Redlands, California, to deliver powerful workman's compensation billing statistics with clear injury focus. A company in Texas wants to examine injury frequency and treatment cost in an effort to review employee safety programs. CorVel uses BodyViewer and client workman's compensation data to analyze these questions.

BodyViewer facilitates the analysis of more than fourteen thousand ICD-9 codes, which are used by the health care industry to index ailments, treatments, and procedures.

BodyViewer maps the results onto an outline of the human body, color-coding parts or representative parts of systems, so that it's easy to see which types of injuries occur most frequently and how much they cost to treat. As is often the case with workman's compensation injuries, musculoskeletal system injuries appear most frequently in this client's billing records.

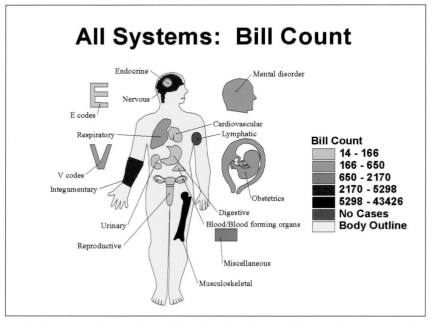

The dark blue on this map shows the type of injury (musculoskeletal) that appears most often in the client's billing records.

Drilling down

Since the musculoskeletal system can be used to describe injuries to the head, neck, arms, back, and legs, analysts use BodyViewer to find the most frequent musculoskeletal injuries by their ICD-9 codes. Injuries to the vertebral column (dark blue) are the most common, accumulating between 9,418 and 15,324 medical bills. Using BodyViewer, analysts create a second, more specific map showing where musculoskeletal injuries occur (in this case, the lower back and spine). Lower- back injuries, often caused by incorrect lifting, are among the most common and most expensive to treat.

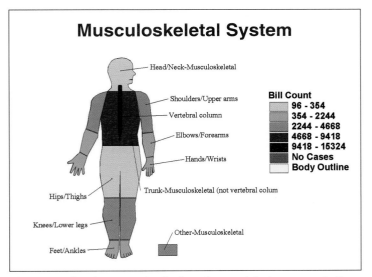

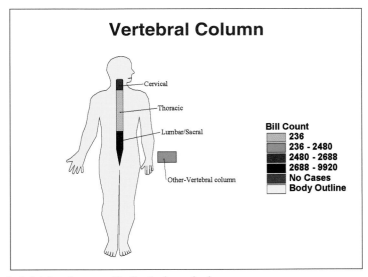

These maps show in greater detail where the most injuries occur—to the musculoskeletal system, specifically the lower back.

From general to specific

Once injury frequency is determined, CorVel analysts use Patient Access (another ArcView GIS extension from GeoHealth) with patient ZIP Code information to create a map of injured workers and network provider locations. Thus, CorVel links patient and network provider proximity, enabling the company to channel injured workers for the most efficient care.

This type of map, as well as that on the following page, are used to bid for client business, or during contract renewal negotiations, and are very effective sales tools for CorVel.

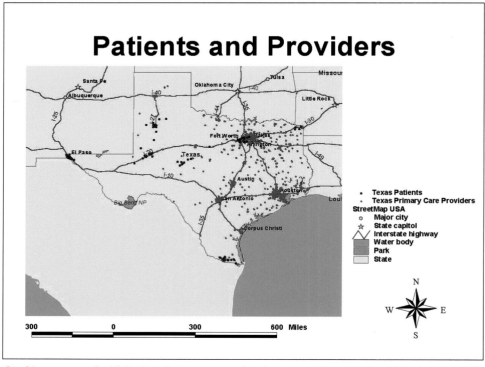

On this map created with Patient Access, patients (employees) are shown in blue, while the network of primary care providers is shown in green.

How close is close?

In another application of Patient Access, a client wants to know how many employees, not just those that have been injured, are within 10 miles of at least two primary care physicians. To determine this, the CorVel analysts create a map showing the distance between each employee and the closest facility.

First, they gather ZIP Code data about the client's employees. They then import this data into ArcView GIS for editing and viewing with Patient Access. The resulting map illustrates employee locations, as well as which provider locations are within 10 miles and which aren't. The green dots represent employees living within 10 miles of at least two physicians.

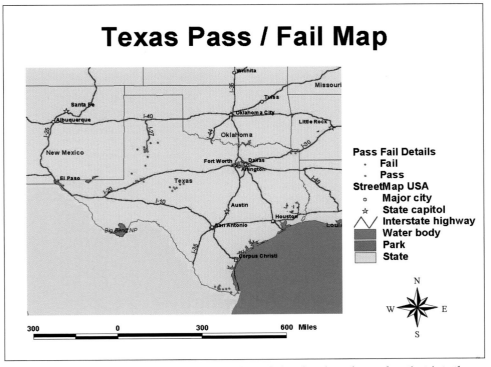

On this map, the distance to providers has been color-coded to show how close each patient is to the nearest provider.

Reporting the facts

The results are exported to ArcView GIS to create summary reports. From these, the client can see that 90 percent of the employees live within 10 miles of at least two CorVel physicians.

The report also includes an employee-specific reference to the nearest provider and the distance to that provider. Similar maps can be created using specific provider types, such as OB/GYNs, pediatricians, or cardiologists.

Armed with these results, the employer not only learns of the need to increase workplace awareness of correct lifting methods to reduce lower back injuries, but also learns that channeling injured employees to CorVel's provider network for treatment will result in maximum savings.

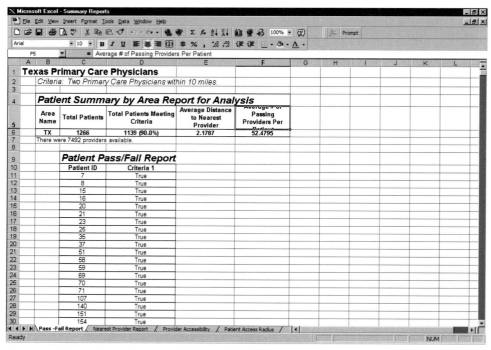

The pass/fail analysis can be imported into ArcView GIS and viewed as a summary report.

The system

Hardware: PC running Windows NT

Software: ArcView GIS; BodyViewer and Patient Access (ArcView GIS extensions)

The data

Proprietary data from clients on patient locations and ailments, street maps, political boundaries, and CorVel's provider location data

The people

Special thanks to Jill Wyland, a GIS specialist at CorVel; Tom Benson, vice president of CorVel; and Dr. Christopher Austin, president of GeoHealth, Inc.

CorVel

Chapter 10

●●●●● Making it even

HEALTH MAINTENANCE ORGANIZATIONS (HMOs) are in the business of providing health care. To contain costs, they contract with physicians and medical groups to provide care at set rates. They then assign patients, called members, to these offices, guaranteeing full rosters.

Sometimes too full. Since members normally use the facility closest to their homes, in densely populated areas, the appointment books quickly fill. When this happens, it's harder for members to make appointments for just a few days away, the doctors are too busy, and the facilities have a difficult time operating within their budgets.

In this chapter, you'll see how Kaiser Permanente, Southern California, uses ArcInfo to assign members to the closest facilities and then monitor enrollment numbers to plan ahead for new locations and to manage funding.

Kaiser Permanente, Southern California, owns and operates 11 hospitals and some 50 medical office buildings over eight counties.

These facilities are grouped into what Kaiser calls medical service areas, comprised of one or more medical centers and satellite medical office buildings. Members are assigned to a service area based on their ZIP Code.

Kaiser uses GIS to assign members and help the HMO monitor how many members are currently assigned to each service area. When a facility is full, Kaiser then uses GIS to find the best location for a new facility and then reassign members.

Unlike at most HMOs, Kaiser's members are free to use whichever southern California "Plan" facility they choose. However, for service planning and budgeting purposes, travel time is employed.

An emerging competitive area for HMOs is accessibility, which means patients can call and make an appointment just a few days away for nonemergencies.

Who goes where?

The population in one Los Angeles County service area is growing so rapidly that customers have been having difficulty making an appointment within a reasonable time, especially at facility A. To determine whether they should build a new primary care facility in this service area, Kaiser's GIS analysts take a closer look at all three service areas.

They use ArcInfo to display the three primary care facilities in this service area and the ZIP Codes assigned to them. The white dots on the map indicate the centroid, or geographic center, of each ZIP Code. These centroids are used to represent polygons, such as ZIP Codes, as points. Measuring distance requires a point-to-point measurement, so using the centroid of a polygon allows for more uniform measurements.

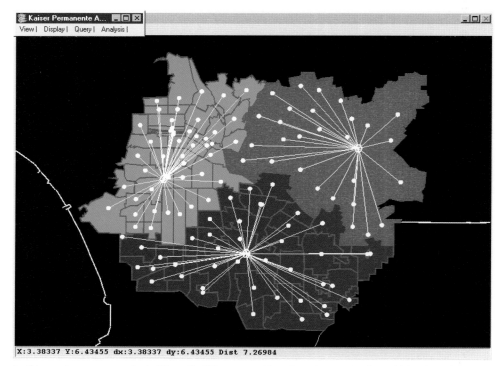

In this service area comprised of three facilities, access times have become too long. Kaiser's analysts are viewing the ZIP Codes assigned to these facilities (A, B, and C) to determine whether a fourth facility is needed.

Too many *whos* at one *where*

The number of members living in the ZIP Codes for each of these facilities is then calculated and displayed. These facilities have about the same number of doctors and are about the same size, but facility A is serving 340,000 members, while B and C serve 150,000 and 165,000 respectively.

Because rapid growth is expected to continue in the ZIP Codes served by A, this analysis indicates that a new center should be opened there.

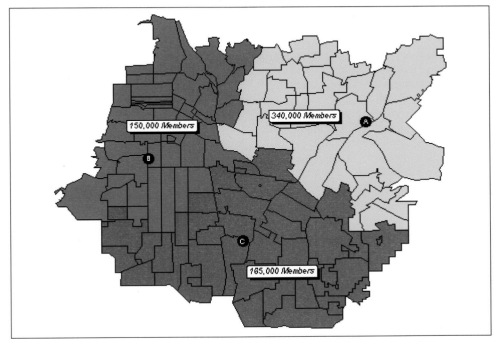

Although the three facilities draw from roughly equal geographic areas, facility A is serving many more members.

Cut and reshuffle

Working with the GIS Department, Kaiser's planners identify several potential sites for a new primary care facility. The planners have studied demographic shifts within this region, and can accurately estimate how many members will be living there in the coming years.

This map shows the proposed site for facility D. Its location, along major roads (see inset), makes it convenient to many of the members now traveling to A or C.

ArcInfo automatically reassigns ZIP Codes, and hence members, to the closest of the four facilities.

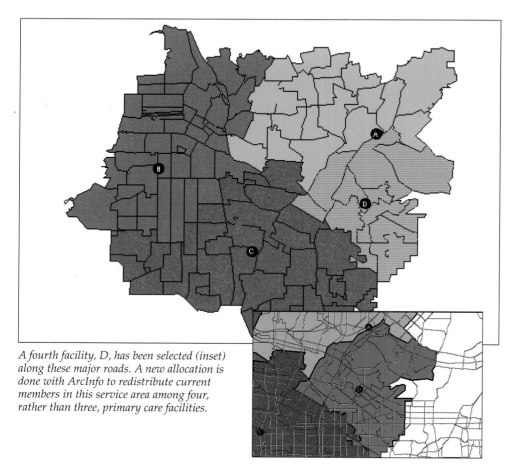

A fourth facility, D, has been selected (inset) along these major roads. A new allocation is done with ArcInfo to redistribute current members in this service area among four, rather than three, primary care facilities.

Restoring balance

As hoped, redistributing the members among the four facilities balances the number of members assigned to each one. Facility A now has 185,000 members while facility C loses just 5,000 members. Membership in facility D is 160,000.

To double-check the reallocation, the analysts next use the GIS to estimate how long members in each ZIP Code must drive to reach their assigned facility. ESRI created this customized "minimum travel time" application for Kaiser. Minimum travel time is Kaiser's guideline for assigning ZIP Codes to primary care facilities. ZIP Code centroids that are closer to one facility than another (based on travel time) are assigned wholly to the closest facility.

This application is used to calculate the travel time from the centroid of each ZIP Code to the assigned facility. In this case, they are all within an acceptable range—15 minutes or less.

The drive-time data from this analysis is added to a spreadsheet to share with service area administrators and planners. This spreadsheet shows the ZIP Codes included in this service area and their drive times, facility assignment (A, B, C, or D), and number of members. This spreadsheet is a reference for administrators when discussing member access, individual facility funding, and long-range expansion plans.

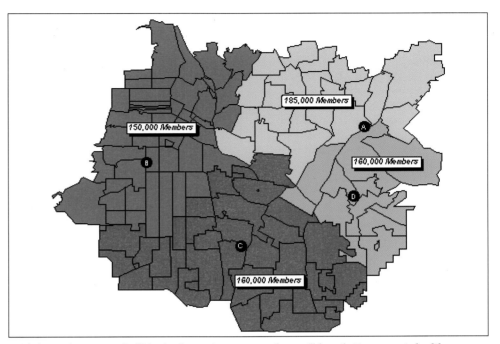

With four primary care facilities in the service area, members will have better access to health care services.

A powerful feature

The GIS and patient data is also used by the analysts to locate specialized services. For example, if Kaiser was interested in opening a birthing center, the company would want to single out demographic data for 15- to 44-year-old females. Using demographics for these people by block group from a data vendor, Kaiser can automatically move the ZIP Code centroid to reflect where these women of child-bearing age live. This is a powerful feature because the centroids, which are normally used to calculate distance in GIS studies, do not necessarily represent where people in the ZIP Code live, or where population segments within the general population live. In large areas with few people, this could throw off the assignment calculations because the people in the area might live nowhere near the centroid, and may in fact be geographically closer to a service area other than the one they were assigned to.

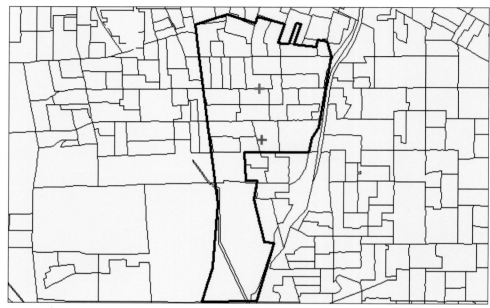

This map shows a single ZIP Code (the thick black boundary) and block groups (the thin black lines). Using census data, the analysts determine where women aged 15 to 44 live. They move the "weight" for this ZIP Code (from red to green) to more accurately represent this population's location within the area.

The system

Hardware: Compaq Deskpro

Software: ArcInfo, Atlas GIS

The data

Kaiser's proprietary patient data, census data, Etak® street data

The people

Special thanks to Robert Pierce, Ph.D., director of the GIS Department at Kaiser Permanente, Southern California.

Chapter 11

•••• Finding a place

HOSPITALS ARE NOT ONLY FILLED WITH PATIENTS and the highly trained professionals who operate the expensive equipment for treating those patients; hospitals are also filled with mountains of information: demographic, clinical, financial, operational, and environmental. All this data about patients and their care, about staff and their capabilities, equipment and its operating history and performance, supplies and their location, and the facilities themselves and their engineering infrastructure, has to be managed each and every day, around the clock.

Having the right information at the right time displayed in a manner that contributes to creating a safe and confident environment for patients and staff alike is what Loma Linda University Medical Center's Patient Location and Care Environment System, or PLACES, is all about.

The 427-bed, 11-floor Loma Linda University Medical Center (LLUMC) is the trauma center for Inyo, Mono, Riverside, and San Bernardino counties in southern California. Its clinical programs for neonatal care, outpatient surgery, and corneal transplants are some of the largest in the United States. It is widely regarded as the world leader for transplanting hearts in infants and for proton radiation. LLUMC, along with its affiliated entities—Loma Linda University Children's Hospital, Loma Linda University Community Medical Center, and Loma Linda University Behavioral Medicine Center—have a total of 880 beds.

Each year Loma Linda University Medical Center admits more than 34,000 patients and serves about half a million outpatients.

Keeping track

While being large and well known has its advantages, it is accompanied by tons of information as patients are checked in, receive treatment, moved from room to room, and discharged.

In 1998, the center's Information Services department used ArcView GIS in a pilot project to develop a system for monitoring where patients are put when they're admitted. Called PLACES, for Patient Location and Care Environment System, the system will help administrators and staff view patient information on monitors showing rooms and beds.

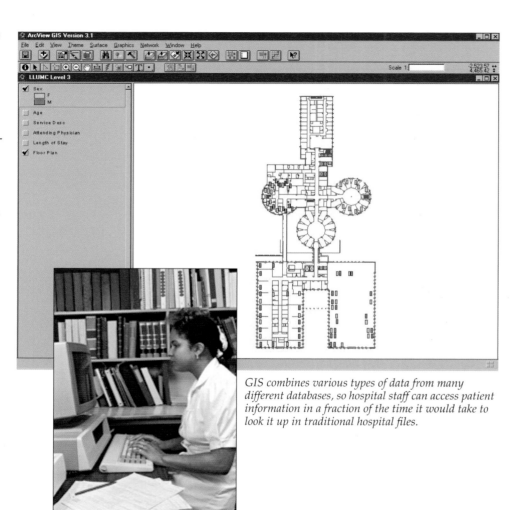

GIS combines various types of data from many different databases, so hospital staff can access patient information in a fraction of the time it would take to look it up in traditional hospital files.

Entering the ward

In the various places throughout the hospital where patients are admitted, staff use the system to check patients in or move them to new rooms.

Logging onto PLACES displays a plan for each floor, showing rooms and beds. Staff members click on-screen tools to view different kinds of patient information.

To make things easier on everyone, the staff tries to pair roommates based on certain criteria, like which condition they have, who the attending physician is, how long they'll be staying, and whether they are male or female. By carefully pairing roommates, they can avoid many complaints. For example, a person with very few visitors may resent the constant stream another patient may have day in and day out. A patient who will be in the hospital for two weeks may not appreciate being paired with a string of roommates who were in for two to three days a piece. Or a mother whose baby is in ICU may have a very hard time with another patient's baby rooming in, with visitors and family raving about how cute the little bundle is.

So when a nurse admits a man in his late thirties for cardiac tests, she examines his information. She sees that he's scheduled to stay in the hospital for one to two days and that he's being treated by Dr. King.

Using the mouse, she clicks on the plan for the cardiac ward on the third floor to view patient data.

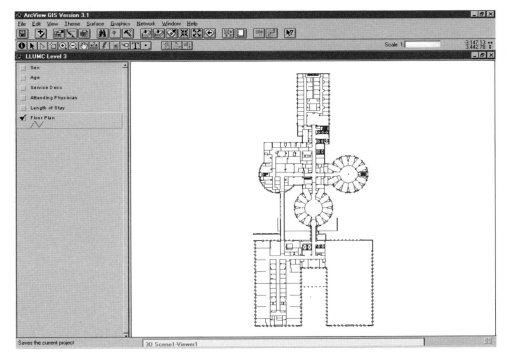

This plan shows the hospital's third floor. Clicking on different themes in the table of contents (left) shows different kinds of information.

Matching roomies

On this map, the nurse sees the occupied beds on this floor color-coded by the time each patient is expected to stay, from one day to ten days.

She's looking for an unoccupied bed in a room with a patient staying one to two days (dark pink). She sees several rooms that would be compatible by length of stay, so she uses PLACES to query those rooms for more information.

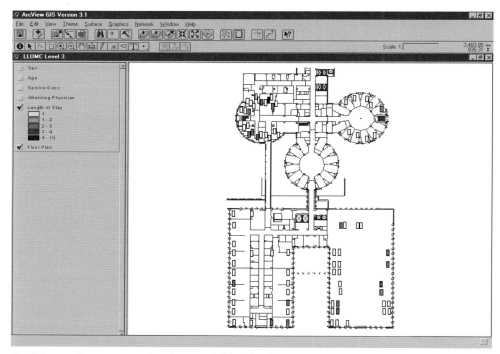

On this map, the nurse can view the occupied beds by the patients' projected length of stay from one day (pink) to ten days (dark red).

The search narrows

The nurse uses PLACES to see if other men staying for a similar length of time are receiving similar treatments. She clicks on *Sex* to view the patients by gender and then on *Service Desc* to see which type of treatment each is in for.

Even if patients have other things in common, the type of treatment they'll receive can sometimes be the deciding factor for placement. For example, a patient admitted for a life-threatening condition probably wouldn't be paired with someone in for routine tests.

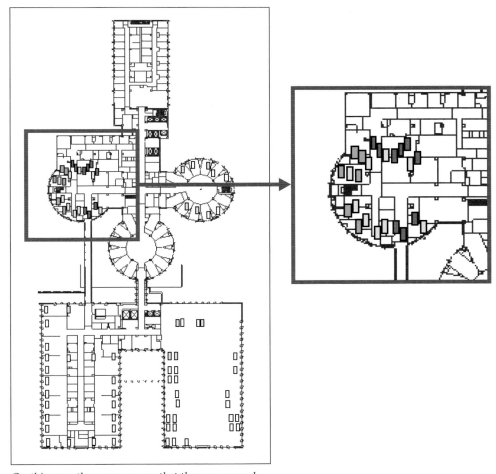

On this map, the nurse can see that there are several rooms with empty beds (yellow). She looks more specifically at the rooms with general cardiac patients (orange) rather than those who are in for surgery (red).

Done

To make a final decision on the best place to put this patient, she uses the system to look at one more piece of patient data—the attending physician. Pairing patients that have the same doctor can also make things easier on the physician.

Just in time too. Because now Dr. King stops by to ask for a list of her patients on the floor. The nurse clicks on *Attending Physician*. Dr. King's patients, shown in dark blue, can be isolated and mapped at her request.

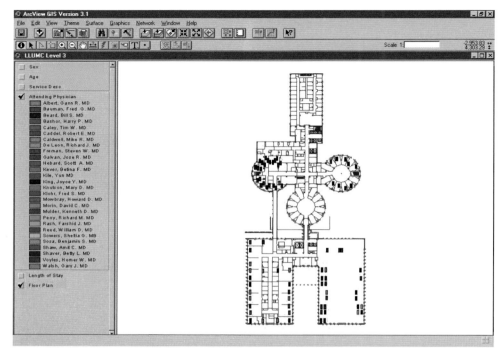

This map shows patients by doctor. The nurse can query the system for patients being treated by one particular doctor, then provide the doctor with a floor map to use during rounds.

Fielding questions

The nursing staff also uses PLACES to answer inquiries from the staff and from families of patients who call to find out room numbers, how their relative or friend is doing, or other information. The system is being improved during 1999 so the doctors will be able to access patient information from their office PCs.

Hospital operators can use PLACES to provide both doctors and patients' family members with information like where a patient is and how long that patient is likely to be in the hospital.

The system

Software: PLACES, ArcView GIS

Hardware: Windows NT server

The data

CAD/CAM floor drawings, real-time patient data

The people

Special thanks to Eugene R. Boyer, director of Business Applications and Development at LLUMC.

Chapter 12

Tracking the plumes

IT'S FOUR O'CLOCK IN THE MORNING on Thursday, the eleventh of April, 1996. In about 15 minutes a train will jump off the rails near Alberton, Montana, releasing lethal levels of chlorine gas. Within minutes of the crash, local firefighters and sheriff's deputies will have swung into action, evacuating the town and surrounding areas. By midday, they're joined by state and federal agencies, including the Centers for Disease Control's Agency for Toxic Substances and Disease Registry (ATSDR), which studies how toxic spills and substances released from hazardous waste sites affect people's health.

Since 1991, the agency has used GIS software to create computer models for its reports, showing how chemicals spread through soil, air, or water, and who and what will be affected. The agency also studies what happens to people who are exposed to hazardous substances. In this chapter, you'll see how the agency used GIS software to model the Alberton spill and help protect people living nearby.

The Agency for Toxic Substances and Disease Registry, the principal federal public health agency for studying hazardous waste sites and spills, responded quickly to the 1996 derailment. Its GIS staff in Atlanta, Georgia, gathered information about the spill, such as what the train was carrying, how much was estimated to have leaked, what the terrain was like, and where the gas would likely spread.

The maps they made showed such important information as where the chemicals are located in relation to people's homes.

When a train derailed near Alberton in 1996, one person died and more than 350 were hospitalized when plumes of chlorine gas escaped.

Photos courtesy of Paul Manson

Understanding the danger

The derailed cars that ruptured sent a cloud of poisonous chlorine gas into the predawn sky. Officials later estimated that 122,000 pounds of chlorine gas escaped from the cars, making this event the second-largest chlorine spill in railroading history.

When chlorine comes in contact with the body's moisture, it turns into hydrochloric acid, which can be deadly. In fact, the one person who died when the train derailed survived the crash, but succumbed from exposure to the chlorine gas while attempting to escape the wreckage.

For healthy adults, the effects of mild exposure—red eyes, a dry cough, and a sore throat—usually clear up within a short time. But for the very young and very old, or for pregnant women or people with lung conditions, exposure to even mild levels of this gas (approximately 0.5 ppm) can be deadly.

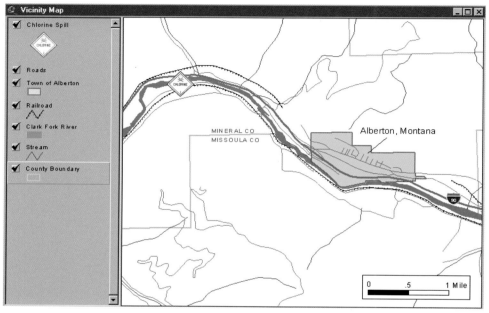

The Alberton derailment, indicated by the diamond symbol, happened in a gorge near the Clark Fork River, not far from the town of Alberton (shown here outlined in red).

Putting people on the map

The GIS staff used census data to look at the town's population and identify where children, elderly people, and women of child-bearing age (15 to 44) lived. These population maps, such as the one at the right showing where the highest density of children under six live, helped them decide who to evacuate and when.

Agency staff helped the state and local health departments interview people evacuated from their homes to see if they were experiencing any symptoms of poisoning and entered this data into the GIS.

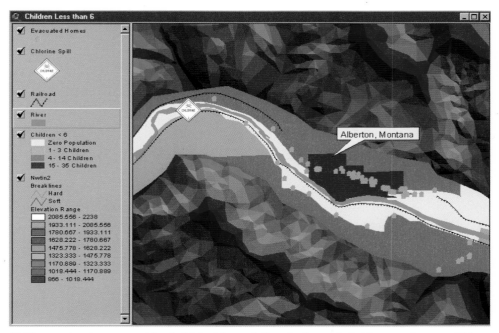

Children under six were considered a high-risk population. As demonstrated here, most young children live in the town, with fewer living near the actual spill site.

Fleeing the slugs

GIS was used by several agencies responding to the spill. To help the evacuation teams, the GIS staff from the EPA went to work to estimate how the chlorine would move through the area. Since chlorine gas is heavier than air, it must be moved by wind. That morning was rainy, with only a light wind, so they realized the chlorine would not move quickly.

But still it moved. As the chlorine pulsed from the wrecked train, it crept in plumes, or slugs, across the Clark Fork River (blue), over Interstate 90, and toward homes. About a thousand people in Alberton and the surrounding area were evacuated and a 49-mile portion of the highway was closed, between the towns of St. Regis and Frenchtown. The interstate was closed for 17 days, the longest closure of an interstate in U.S. history.

As the public health agency involved, ATSDR focused on the interview study of the people who had been evacuated. Back at ATSDR's home office in Atlanta, analysts used the GIS to overlay information about the site as reports came in, creating maps the interview teams could use to track the progress of the slugs and to estimate the size of the potentially exposed population.

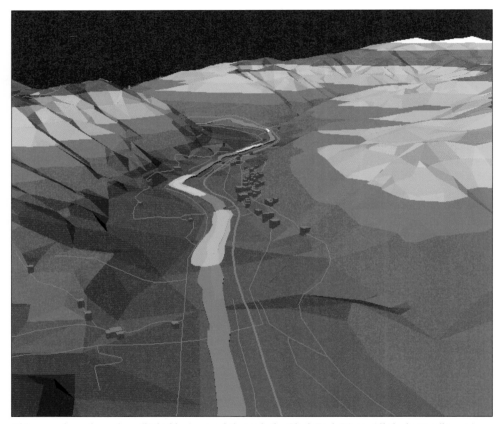

This map shows how slugs (light blue) moved through the Clark Fork River. All the homes (brown) within about 7 square miles in western Montana, near the Idaho border, were evacuated.

Dissecting the slugs

As the slugs moved slowly through the canyon, their upper levels quickly evaporated. An ATSDR atmospheric scientist specializing in plume movement prediction used a gas-dispersion algorithm to map how the chlorine slugs would continue to move through the canyon and how long they would take to dissipate.

The analysts in Atlanta then used ArcView 3D Analyst™, an ArcView GIS extension, to calculate and display the complex three-dimensional surfaces of the canyon walls and terrain.

These results were mapped with ArcInfo to show the locations and movement of the slugs in a realistic context.

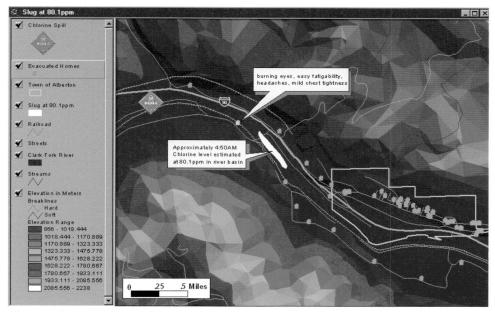

This map shows the location of the slug at approximately 4:50 A.M., 35 minutes after the wreck. The estimated dilution of chlorine in the river basin is 80.1 ppm. Residents evacuated from surrounding homes (orange) reported burning eyes, fatigue, headaches, and chest tightness.

Recording symptoms

While contamination experts modeled the terrain and the slugs, other experts were working on what health effects to expect throughout the basin.

They used ArcInfo to geocode people's addresses so they could see where sensitive people lived—such as an elderly couple or a family with small children. Since exposure to chlorine gas varies by its concentration, it was important to record the symptoms from people at these locations. By recording each person's symptoms alongside their address, the modelers were able to estimate how much chlorine was in the air at that location.

After the initial danger passed, the analysts used this data with ArcView GIS to understand more about the movement of chlorine gas. They were able to see how it varied from their expectations, where it was less concentrated or more concentrated than they thought it would be, how long it took to reach a certain location, and whether the symptoms of people living there differed from what was expected.

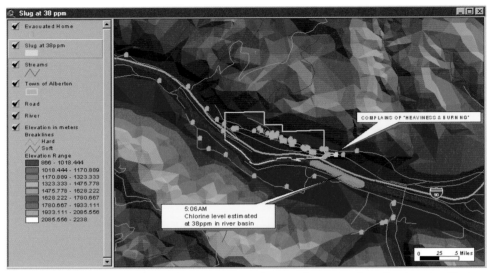

This map shows the location of the slug at 5:06 A.M., about one hour after the spill, when the chlorine levels were estimated at 33 ppm. The analysts can click on houses to see occupants' symptoms.

Drawing conclusions

To demonstrate how this data can be used to improve future responses, the analysts query with ArcInfo to display only homes inside a 1-mile buffer of the spill and create maps about the people living there.

The 1-mile buffer shows the homes exposed to the highest levels of the gas. Using ArcInfo, the analysts can summarize how many people are in this area and their demographic breakdown, and conduct analyses about population segments and their reported symptoms.

By learning all they can about the effects of a spill, both immediate and long-term, analysts are better able to predict and possibly minimize the effects of a similar spill in the future.

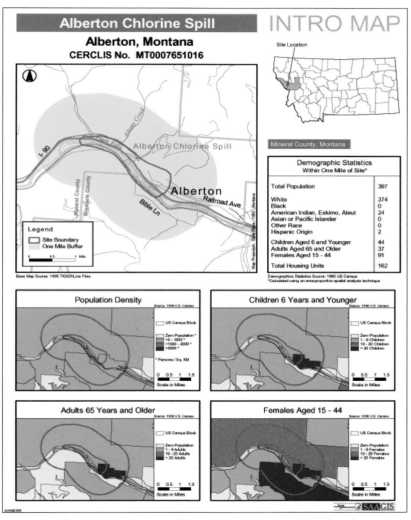

The Agency for Toxic Substances and Disease Registry gives all health assessors responding to a hazardous waste site or spill a standard demographic map like this so they can hit the ground running.

Public access

By the end of 1999, the agency hopes to make information about toxic spills like Alberton's available at its Web site (www.atsdr.cdc.gov), using MapObjects to let visitors query and map data.

Visitors will be able to view information from several sample projects and use the MapObjects query tools to create custom maps with the data much like the demographics map shown on page 99.

The system

Hardware: Dell 610 servers, Windows NT workstations, Sun SPARC 10 workstations

Software: ArcView GIS, ArcInfo, Spatial Database Engine™ (SDE®), MapObjects, SLAB model

The data

Topography, hydrology, vegetation, land-use, PRIZM®/Claritas® demographics, digital elevation models, resident-survey (health conditions), and National Weather Services meteorological data.

The people

Thanks to ATSDR's Dr. Susan Metcalf, Dr. Virginia Lee, Greg Zarus, and Dr. Janet Heitgerd; Dr. Chris Weiss, of Region VIII EPA; Paul Calame, a GIS analyst at EDS who works in Atlanta with the CDC; and Danika Holm, consultant.

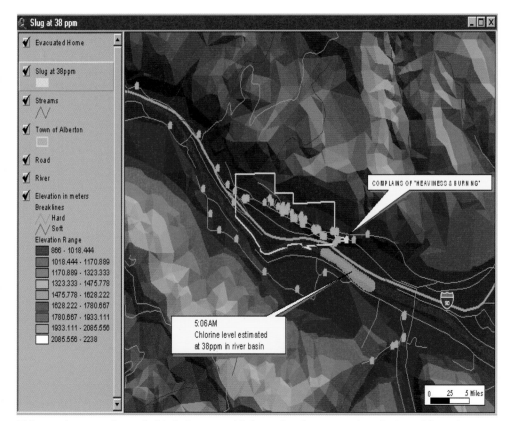

This sample screen shows the kind of maps and information the agency plans for its public Web site.

Other books from ESRI Press

ESRI Special Editions

GIS for Everyone
Now everyone can create smart maps for school, work, home, or community action using a personal computer. Includes the ArcExplorer™ geographic data viewer and more than 500 megabytes of geographic data. ISBN 1-879102-49-8

The ESRI Guide to GIS Analysis
By the author of the best-selling GIS classic *Zeroing In: GIS at Work in the Community* comes an important new book about how to do real analysis with a geographic information system. *The ESRI Guide to GIS Analysis, Volume 1: Geographic Patterns and Relationships* focuses on six of the most common geographic analysis tasks. ISBN 1-879102-06-4

Modeling Our World
With this comprehensive guide and reference to GIS data modeling and to the new geodatabase model introduced with ArcInfo 8, you'll learn how to make the right decisions about modeling data, from database design and data capture to spatial analysis and visual presentation. ISBN 1-879102-62-5

ESRI Map Book: Implementing Concepts of Geography
A full-color collection of some of the finest maps produced using GIS software. ISBN 1-879102-60-9

The Case Studies Series

ArcView GIS Means Business
Written for business professionals, this book is a behind-the-scenes look at how some of America's most successful companies have used desktop GIS technology. The book is loaded with full-color illustrations and comes with a trial copy of ArcView GIS software and a GIS tutorial. ISBN 1-879102-51-X

Zeroing In: Geographic Information Systems at Work in the Community
In twelve "tales from the digital map age," this book shows how people use GIS in their daily jobs. An accessible and engaging introduction to GIS for anyone who deals with geographic information. ISBN 1-879102-50-1

Serving Maps on the Internet
Take an insider's look at how today's forward-thinking organizations distribute map-based information via the Internet. Case studies cover a range of applications for ArcView Internet Map Server technology from ESRI. This book should interest anyone who wants to publish geospatial data on the World Wide Web. ISBN 1-879102-52-8

Managing Natural Resources with GIS
Find out how GIS technology helps people design solutions to such pressing challenges as wildfires, urban blight, air and water degradation, species endangerment, disaster mitigation, coastline erosion, and public education. The experiences of public and private organizations provide real-world examples. ISBN 1-879102-53-6

MORE ESRI PRESS TITLES ARE LISTED ON THE NEXT PAGE

ESRI educational products cover topics related to geographic information science, GIS applications, and ESRI technology. You can choose among instructor-led courses, Web-based courses, and self-study workbooks to find education solutions that fit your learning style and pocketbook. Visit **www.esri.com/education** *for more information.*

ESRI Press ■ 380 New York Street ■ Redlands, California 92373-8100

Other books from ESRI Press

The Case Studies Series CONTINUED

Enterprise GIS for Energy Companies
A volume of case studies showing how electric and gas utilities use geographic information systems to manage their facilities more cost effectively, find new market opportunities, and better serve their customers. ISBN 1-879102-48-X

Transportation GIS
From monitoring rail systems and airplane noise levels, to making bus routes more efficient and improving roads, this book describes how geographic information systems have emerged as the tool of choice for transportation planners. ISBN 1-879102-47-1

GIS for Landscape Architects
From Karen Hanna, noted landscape architect and GIS pioneer, comes GIS for Landscape Architects. Through actual examples, you'll learn how landscape architects, land planners, and designers now rely on GIS to create visual frameworks within which spatial data and information are gathered, interpreted, manipulated, and shared. ISBN 1-879102-64-1

GIS for Health Organizations
Health management is a rapidly developing field, where even slight shifts in policy affect the health care we receive. In this book, you'll see how physicians, public health officials, insurance providers, hospitals, epidemiologists, researchers, and HMO executives use GIS to focus resources to meet the needs of those in their care. ISBN 1-879102-65-X

ESRI Software Workbooks

Understanding GIS: The ARC/INFO Method (UNIX/Windows NT version)
A hands-on introduction to geographic information system technology. Designed primarily for beginners, this classic text guides readers through a complete GIS project in ten easy-to-follow lessons. ISBN 1-879102-01-3

Understanding GIS: The ARC/INFO Method (PC version)
ISBN 1-879102-00-5

ARC Macro Language: Developing Menus and Macros with AML
ARC Macro Language (AML™) software gives you the power to tailor workstation ArcInfo software's geoprocessing operations to specific applications. This workbook teaches AML in the context of accomplishing practical workstation ArcInfo tasks, and presents both basic and advanced techniques. ISBN 1-879102-18-8

Getting to Know ArcView GIS
A colorful, nontechnical introduction to GIS technology and ArcView GIS software, this workbook comes with a working ArcView GIS demonstration copy. Follow the book's scenario-based exercises or work through them using the CD and learn how to do your own ArcView GIS project. ISBN 1-879102-46-3

Extending ArcView GIS
This sequel to the award-winning Getting to Know ArcView GIS is written for those who understand basic GIS concepts and are ready to extend the analytical power of the core ArcView GIS software. The book consists of short conceptual overviews followed by detailed exercises framed in the context of real problems. ISBN 1-879102-05-6

ESRI Press publishes a growing list of GIS-related books. Ask for these books at your local bookstore or order by calling 1-800-447-9778. You can also shop online at www.esri.com/gisstore. Outside the United States, contact your local ESRI distributor.

ESRI Press ■ 380 New York Street ■ Redlands, California 92373-8100